f3

Quick Cook!

MARSHALL CAVENDISH

This edition exclusive to Dealerfield Limited
Martin Close, Blenheim Estate, Bulwell
Nottingham NG8 8UV.

Produced by Marshall Cavendish Books, London
(a division of Marshall Cavendish Partworks Ltd.)
Copyright © Marshall Cavendish Limited 1997
This Edition printed 1997

ISBN 1-85435-887-1

British Library Cataloguing in Publication Data:
A catalogue record for this book is available from the British Library

Marshall Cavendish Editorial Staff
Managing Editor: Ellen Dupont
Editor: Susie Dawson
Designer: Tim Brown
Production: Craig Chubb

Printed in Dubai, U.A.E.

CONTENTS

STARTERS

When deciding on your menu, be sure to choose a starter that will complement your choice of main course and dessert. With the right balance, any of these mouthwatering starters will transform a simple supper into a dinner party in one easy stroke.

MEXICAN GUACAMOLE

SERVES 4
20 MINS TO PREPARE

1 beef tomato or
2 large tomatoes
4 spring onions
1 green chilli
1 garlic clove
3 small or
2 large avocados

1 tbls lemon
or lime juice
1 tbls chopped fresh
coriander, plus
extra to garnish
1 tsp paprika salt
and pepper

1 Put the tomato in a bowl and cover with boiling water. Leave for 2 minutes. Remove and, if the skins have not split, pierce with a fork or skewer. Peel away the skins, cut into quarters and de-seed, then chop. Cut off the green parts of the spring onion and discard. Finely slice the white parts. Using rubber gloves, de-seed and finely chop the chilli. Finely chop the garlic.

2 Halve and peel the avocados, then remove the stones. Roughly chop the flesh and place in a blender or food processor, then immediately add the lemon or lime juice, tomato, spring onion, chilli, garlic, coriander and paprika.

3 Process quickly until the ingredients are well mixed but not completely smooth. Season with salt and pepper to taste, garnish with coriander and serve at once.

COOK'S TIPS

The citrus juice is an important part of this recipe — it should be added immediately after the avocados because it helps to prevent them turning brown once they have been cut open. Guacamole is best made immediately before serving but, if you are making it in advance, you can slow down discoloration by leaving one of the avocado stones in the dip – just don't forget to remove the stone before serving! Another tip is to drizzle a tablespoon of olive oil over the guacamole, covering the surface.

VEGETABLE APPETIZER WITH TWO DIPS

SERVES 4
30 MINS TO PREPARE

½ green pepper,
seeded
½ red pepper,
seeded
2 carrots
1 head of chicory
7.5cm/3 in
cucumber
12 button
mushrooms
watercress sprig,
to garnish

FOR HERBED CHEESE DIP:
175g/6oz
cottage cheese
4 tbls soured cream
1 tbls lemon juice
4 tbls finely
snipped chives
salt and pepper

FOR THE ANCHOVY DIP:
50g/2 oz canned
anchovy fillets, drained
1 garlic clove, crushed
3 tbls olive oil
1 tsp lemon juice
3 tbls mayonnaise
3 tbls double cream
paprika

1 To make the herbed cheese dip, blend the cottage cheese, soured cream and lemon juice in a food processor or electric blender until smooth. Reserve some chives to garnish, stir the rest into the mixture and season to taste with the remaining salt and pepper. Transfer to a serving bowl and sprinkle the remaining chives over the top. Cover and chill until ready to serve.

2 To make the anchovy dip, place the drained anchovy fillets and the garlic in a small bowl or mortar and pound to a pulp. Add the olive oil, lemon juice, mayonnaise and cream, mix well and season with pepper to taste. Transfer to a serving bowl and sprinkle with paprika. Cover and chill until ready to serve.

3 Wash all the vegetables and pat dry with kitchen towels. Cut the green and red pepper halves into strips. Peel and cut each carrot into strips. Separate the chicory leaves. Slice the piece of cucumber.

4 Just before serving, group all the vegetables around the outside of a serving platter, and place the two bowls of dips in the centre. Alternatively, place the vegetables in colourful clumps in a basket, and serve the two bowls of dip beside it.

GARLIC MUSHROOMS
IN RED WINE

SERVES 4
15 MINS TO PREPARE • 20 MINS TO COOK

450g/1lb mixed
chestnut and button
mushrooms
3 tbls olive oil
1 small onion,
finely chopped
4 garlic cloves,
crushed
150ml/5fl oz
dry red wine

2 tbls chopped fresh
thyme or 2
tsp dried
1 tsp soft dark
brown sugar
salt and pepper
fresh thyme,
to garnish
(optional)

1 Use a piece of damp kitchen towel to wipe the mushrooms thoroughly, then cut them in half with a small, sharp knife. It is not necessary to trim the stems unless they are very dirty.

2 Heat the oil in a large saucepan. Add the onion and garlic and fry over medium heat for 2–3 minutes or until the onion is slightly soft, stirring frequently. Add the mushrooms and stir until they have absorbed all the the oil

3 Pour in the wine, then stir in the thyme, sugar and salt and pepper to taste until well blended. Leave to simmer, uncovered, for 10 minutes, stirring occasionally.

4 Serve in soup plates, garnished with fresh thyme, if wished, and with plenty of bread to soak up the juices.

SMOKED MACKEREL
PÂTÉ IN LEMON CASES

SERVES 6
20 MINS TO PREPARE

225g/½lb
mackerel fillets
400g/14oz low-fat
soft cheese
2 tsp creamed
horseradish sauce
1 tbls lemon juice
pepper

6 lemons
paprika and dill
sprigs, to garnish
savoury crackers
or toast, to serve

1 Peel away the skin from the mackerel fillets, loosening the edge of the skin with the point of a knife, if necessary. Break each fillet into small pieces, removing any bones, and put into a bowl.

2 Add the cheese, horseradish sauce, lemon juice and a generous sprinkling of pepper to the mackerel and, using a fork, mash together until the mixture is creamy.

3 Cut the tops off the lemons and, with a teaspoon, scoop out the flesh and reserve the tops as lids. (You won't need the flesh for this recipe, but why not use it for fresh lemonade?) Cut a small bit off the bottom of each lemon so that it can stand upright. Fill each lemon with the pâté, garnish with a sprinkling of paprika and sprigs of dill and perch the lids on top. Serve with crackers or toast.

MUSSELS IN DRY CIDER

SERVES 4
20 MINS TO PREPARE • 15 MINS TO COOK

3L/5½pt mussels
5 tbls chopped
* shallots*
275ml/½pt
* dry cider*
1 tbls lemon juice
1 tbls chopped
* parsley stems*
1 bouquet garni

50g/2oz unsalted
* butter*
2 tbls chopped
* parsley*
freshly ground black
* pepper*
flat leaf parsley, to
* garnish*

1 Scrub the mussels with a stiff brush under cold running water, removing any beards and discarding any mussels which are not firmly closed.

2 Put the shallots, cider, lemon juice, parsley stems and bouquet garni in a large saucepan (not aluminium because of its toxic reaction with lemon juice) and stir. Heat on the hob until boiling, then reduce the heat and simmer for 2 minutes.

3 Add the cleaned mussels to the pan and cover. Turn the heat up and leave the mussels to steam in the liquid for about 8 minutes, stirring frequently with a large wooden spoon.

4 Tip the mussels into a colander and drain the liquid into a bowl. Leave the liquid to stand for 2 minutes so that the sediment settles, then ladle the mussels into four large soup bowls. Check to make sure that all the mussels are open and discard any which are not. Carefully pour the liquid back into the pan, leaving any sediment behind in the bowl. Boil the liquor for 3 minutes, beating in the butter with a fork. Stir in the chopped parsley.

5 Add some freshly ground black pepper, then ladle the liquor over the mussels in the bowls. Garnish with flat leaf parsley.

WHAT TO DRINK

With cider in the cooking liquor, it is an appropriate drink to serve with the dish. If you want to serve wine with the dish for a special occasion, you could serve a crisp, dry, fruity white wine such as a Muscadet de Sèvres-et-Maine sur lie.

PRAWN & AVOCADO
COCKTAIL

SERVES 4
15 MINS TO PREPARE

*150ml/5fl oz
soured cream
150ml/5fl oz
mayonnaise
2 tsp tomato purée
2 tbls chopped
fresh chives
1 garlic clove,
crushed*

*350g/12oz
large peeled,
cooked prawns
2 avocados
1 tbls lemon juice
salt and pepper
chives and lemon
wedges, to garnish
(optional)*

1 Put the soured cream, mayonnaise and tomato purée into a mixing bowl and stir together until well blended and smooth. Stir in the chives and the garlic, then the prawns.

2 Cut the avocados in half and remove and discard the stones. Scoop out the flesh and dice roughly. Turn into a bowl and sprinkle with the lemon juice. Using a wooden spoon, gently turn the diced avocado in the lemon juice; this will prevent it going brown.

3 Add the avocado to the prawn mixture and stir carefully but thoroughly. Taste and add salt and pepper, if wished. Turn this mixture into individual serving dishes and garnish with chives and lemon wedges. Serve at once.

SERVING IDEAS

This makes a good-sized starter or lunchtime snack for four people, though if you're serving it as part of a substantial meal, it could stretch to feed six. For a different presentation, serve it in the halved avocado shells. In this case, brush the flesh remaining in the shells with lemon juice to prevent discoloration.

APPLE & CELERY SALAD

SERVES 4-6 • 20 MINS TO PREPARE

**small head of celery
3 red apples
2 tbls lemon juice
100g/4oz
     walnut pieces
chopped celery
     leaves, to garnish**

**FOR THE DRESSING:
1 garlic clove
2 tbls cider vinegar
salt and freshly
     ground black
     pepper
3 tbls corn oil
3 tbls walnut oil
75g/3oz
     Roquefort cheese**

WHAT TO DRINK

Try a German Riesling with this salad. Its flavour will suit the fruity apple and fresh vegetable flavours, as well as complementing the salty savouriness of the Roquefort cheese.

1 Wash the celery and cut it into 6mm/¼in slices.

2 Leaving the skin on the apples, quarter them, remove the cores and slice. Toss in a bowl with lemon juice to prevent them from browning.

3 Crush and finely chop the garlic. Place in a bowl with the vinegar, salt and pepper. Add the oils a tablespoon at a time, beating well after each addition, to form a thickened dressing.

4 Crumble the cheese into the dressing, then beat until smooth.

5 Put the celery, apples and walnut pieces in a serving bowl, pour the dressing over the top and toss lightly to mix. Garnish with chopped celery leaves. Serve as soon as possible after making.

DANISH CARAWAY SALAD

SERVES 4-6
20 MINS TO PREPARE

1 red apple
1 tbls lemon juice
4 celery sticks
100g/4oz seedless
*   white grapes*
200g/7oz
*   white cabbage*

3 tbls mayonnaise
3 tbls soured cream
1 tbls olive oil
2 tsp caraway seeds
50g/2oz Danish Blue
*   cheese*

WHAT TO DRINK

Crunchy and refreshing, this salad with its caraway seed dressing and garnish of tangy blue cheese would go very well with a glass of chilled Bulgarian Sauvignon Blanc.

1 Peel and core the apple then cut it into cubes and put in a large serving bowl. Sprinkle with the lemon juice.

2 Trim and slice 2 of the celery sticks and add to the bowl. Halve the grapes and add them to the bowl, then mix well.

3 Finely chop the cabbage and add to the bowl. Stir well to mix the ingredients.

4 Combine the mayonnaise, soured cream and olive oil in a bowl. Stir in the caraway seeds.

5 Pour the dressing over the salad ingredients in the serving bowl and toss well.

6 Crumble the blue cheese over the top of the salad and serve garnished with the remaining celery sticks.

THREE-BEAN SALAD

SERVES 4 - 6
20 MINS TO PREPARE

400g/14oz tin black beans
400g/14oz tin red kidney beans
400g/14oz tin chickpeas
1 yellow pepper, seeded
2 tbls chopped parsley
6 spring onions, chopped
3 celery sticks, chopped

FOR THE DRESSING:
3 tbls olive oil
1 tbls lemon juice
1 tsp wholegrain mustard
½ tsp honey
salt and pepper

1 Cut the pepper into quarters lengthwise. Grill under high heat until the skin is blistered and blackened. Put the pepper quarters in a polythene bag, seal and leave to cool, then peel away the skin and slice the pepper. Mix the drained beans and pepper strips together in a bowl.

2 Whisk together the oil, lemon juice, mustard, honey and salt and pepper to taste and pour over the beans.

3 Add the parsley, spring onions and celery to the beans and toss together gently. Adjust the seasoning and serve.

VARIATIONS

Any combination of tinned beans can be used to make this salad which is suitable for vegetarians.

Accompanied with fresh crusty bread to mop up the dressing, it could be served as a healthy vegetarian main course.

MOZZARELLA & TOMATO SALAD

SERVES 6
10 MINS TO PREPARE

500g/1lb ripe
  tomatoes
1 tbls chopped
  fresh parsley
1 tbls chopped
  fresh basil
pinch of sugar

salt and freshly
  ground black
  pepper
175g/6oz
  mozzarella
  cheese
3 tbls black olives
4 tbls olive oil

1 Slice the tomatoes into 5mm/¼in slices. Arrange the slices in an overlapping circular pattern around a flat serving dish. Sprinkle the herbs and sugar over the top and season with salt and pepper to taste.

2 Slice the cheese the same thickness as the tomato slices. Arrange the cheese slices in the centre of the tomatoes. Scatter the olives over.

3 Just before serving, pour over the olive oil and, using a fork, gently lift up the tomato slices so that the oil drains through to them. Serve at once.

INGREDIENTS GUIDE

Mozzarella cheese comes from southern Italy. Originally made from buffalo's milk, but nowadays usually made with cow's milk, it is soft and moist and has a mild flavour.

MAIN COURSES

*Cooking for the family, or entertaining guests,
is quick and easy with these stylish main courses.
This collection of recipes makes the most of fresh
ingredients and simple techniques
– some dishes can be ready in under 15 minutes.*

VEAL CHOP NORMANDY

SERVES 4
10 MINS TO PREPARE • 20 MINS TO COOK

2 firm dessert apples
75g/3oz butter
1 tbls olive oil
salt and freshly
*   ground black*
*   pepper*
4 veal loin chops
100g/4oz peeled
*   baby onions*

100g/4oz button
*   mushrooms, thickly*
*   sliced*
4 tbls Calvados
200ml/7fl oz
*   crème fraîche*
fresh parsley, to
*   garnish (optional)*

1 Peel, core and quarter the apples, then cut each quarter in half lengthways. Melt 25g/1 oz of the butter in a large, heavy-based frying pan and fry the apples gently until soft and golden. Remove the apples from the pan with a slotted spoon and put on a plate.

2 Melt the remaining butter in the frying pan with the oil. Season the chops well, turn up the heat and add them to the pan. Sear the chops for 30 seconds per side, then remove the pan from the heat.

3 When the butter has cooled down, put the pan back over low heat. Add the onions and fry gently, stirring all the time. Four minutes later, add the mushrooms. Cover, then simmer the chops for about 15 minutes.

4 Remove the chops, onions and mushrooms from the pan to a warm serving dish. Turn the heat up under the pan, then add the Calvados and set it alight by carefully passing a naked flame over the centre of the pan. As soon as the flames have died away, add the crème fraîche. Stir the sauce, gently scraping the pan with a wooden spatula or spoon to incorporate any crusty bits.

5 Meanwhile, arrange the chops on warm serving plates. When the sauce has reduced and thickened, spoon it over the chops, and place the mushrooms and onions on top. Return the apple pieces to the pan for 2 minutes to heat them through, then garnish each chop with the apple pieces and fresh parsley.

PEPPERED STEAKS IN MUSTARD SAUCE

SERVES 4
10 MINS TO PREPARE • 15 MINS TO COOK

4 tsp black
*   peppercorns*
4 x 150g/5oz
*   beef steaks*
1 tbls vegetable oil

FOR THE SAUCE:
2 tbls brandy
2 garlic cloves,
*   crushed*
4 tsp wholegrain
*   mustard*
4 tbls double cream

1 Roughly crush the peppercorns using a pestle and mortar or with the end of a rolling pin in a mixing bowl and place in a shallow non-metallic dish. Put the steaks into the dish, turning each one in the peppercorns until completely coated. Cover and set aside until you are ready to cook them.

2 Heat the oil in a large frying pan. Seal the peppered steaks by frying over high heat for 1 minute on each side. Lower the heat to medium and continue cooking for 5 minutes on each side for medium steaks. (Rare steaks will take 3 minutes each side, well-done 8 minutes.) Remove the steaks from the pan and keep warm.

3 Pour the brandy into a ladle and then tip into the frying pan; heat over medium heat until it bubbles. Stand at arm's length and carefully light the brandy with a taper or long match. Wait till the flames die down, then add the garlic, mustard and cream. Allow the sauce to come to the boil, stirring constantly. Serve immediately, poured over the steaks.

PAN-FRIED STEAKS IN BEER

SERVES 4
20 MINS TO PREPARE • 20 MINS TO COOK

2 thick sirloin steaks,
    325-350g/11-12 oz
    each
30ml/2tbls olive oil
1 garlic clove, finely
    chopped
salt
freshly ground black
    pepper

FOR THE SAUCE:
350g/12oz small
    mushrooms, sliced
40g/1½oz butter
15ml/1 tbls lemon
    juice
15ml/1 tbls flour
150ml/5 fl oz lager
5-10ml/1-2 tsp soy
    sauce

1 Cut the steaks in half and brush them with olive oil. Then sprinkle them with the finely chopped garlic, the salt and the freshly ground black pepper to taste. Set aside while you make the sauce.

2 To prepare the sauce, sauté the sliced mushrooms in 40g/1½oz butter and the lemon juice for about 5 minutes. Add the flour to the pan, stirring constantly until well blended, then pour in the lager and, continuing to stir, bring the mixture to the boil.

3 Boil the sauce for 1 minute. Add the soy sauce, and the remaining chopped garlic, and season to taste with freshly ground black pepper. Keep warm.

4 Heat the remaining oil in a frying pan and fry the steaks on each side (3½ minutes for rare, 4–5 minutes for medium and 6–7 minutes for well-done).

5 Either place the steaks on a heated serving dish or leave them in the frying pan. Pour the hot mushroom and beer sauce over the meat and serve as soon as possible.

STIR-FRIED BEEF STRIPS

SERVES 4 - 6
25 MINS TO PREPARE • 5 MINS TO COOK

**350g/12oz beef
steak (fillet or
close-grained
sirloin)
2.5cm/1in cube of
fresh ginger, peeled
and grated
3 garlic cloves,
crushed
1 tbls dark soy sauce
2 tbls dry sherry (or
Chinese rice wine)
salt and pepper
2 tbls corn oil
1 bunch spring
onions, cut into
4cm/1½in lengths**

**100g/4oz bean
sprouts, washed
and trimmed
3 tbls black bean
sauce
1 mango, peeled and
cut into slices
1 red chilli, de-seeded
and sliced into
strips, to garnish
lime segments, to
garnish**

1 Cut the beef fillet into thin slices, approximately 1x4cm/½x1½in. Put in a small bowl and add the ginger, the garlic, the soy sauce, sherry and a little salt and pepper. Leave to marinate for about 15 minutes, turning occasionally.

2 Heat a wok or large, heavy-based frying pan, then add the oil and heat until it is smoking. Lift the beef out of the marinade, toss it into the hot, seasoned oil and stir-fry for about 1 minute. Add the spring onions and fry for a further minute. Add the bean sprouts and the marinade and fry for another couple of minutes.

3 Stir the black bean sauce into the beef mixture and stir vigorously for 60 seconds.

4 Toss in the slices of mango, stir for a couple of seconds then serve immediately, garnished with strips of red chilli and lime segments.

NUTRITION NOTES

Fillets are one of the least fatty cuts of beef, which is rich in iron and the B vitamins. The bean sprouts add fibre to the dish.

EASY CHILLI CON CARNE

SERVES 4
15 MINS TO PREPARE • 30 MINS TO COOK

2 tbls vegetable oil
1 large onion,
  finely chopped
1 green pepper,
  de-seeded and
  chopped
1 red pepper,
  de-seeded and
  chopped
2 tsp hot chilli
  powder
2 tsp ground cumin
600g/1¼lb lean
  minced beef

2 tbls tomato purée
400g/14oz tin
  chopped tomatoes
400g/14oz tin
  red kidney beans,
  drained and rinsed
salt and pepper
275ml/10fl oz
  soured cream
snipped fresh chives,
  to garnish

1 Heat the oil in a large frying pan over medium heat. Add the onion and peppers and fry, stirring frequently, for 5 minutes or until softened but not browned. Stir in the chilli powder and cumin and continue to cook, stirring often, for 2–3 minutes.

2 Add the minced beef to the pan and mix with the other ingredients, using a spatula to break it up. Increase the heat to high and cook, stirring occasionally, for 5 minutes or until the meat is well browned. Spoon off any excess fat.

3 Add the tomato purée and stir until well blended. Stir in the tomatoes and the red kidney beans. Bring the mixture to the boil, then reduce the heat to low. Partially cover the pan and simmer for 10 minutes until the meat and vegetables are tender. Season with salt and pepper to taste. Pour the soured cream into a bowl and garnish with a sprinkling of chives; serve with the hot chilli.

SERVING IDEAS

Chilli con Carne is an ideal dish for parties because it can be made a day ahead and reheated just before serving. Serve with a selection of toppings and let guests add their own, such as finely grated Cheddar cheese, plain Greek-style yogurt or finely diced avocado tossed with a little lemon juice.

TAGLIATELLE ALLA BOLOGNESE

SERVES 4
10 MINS TO PREPARE • 25 MINS TO COOK

2 tbls olive oil
350g/12oz tagliatelle
Parmesan cheese,
  to serve (optional)
parsley sprigs,
  to garnish

FOR THE BOLOGNESE SAUCE:
25g/1oz butter

1 large onion,
  finely chopped
225g/½lb lean
  minced beef
¼ tsp dried
  mixed herbs
150ml/5fl oz
  dry white wine
3 tbls tomato purée
salt and pepper

1 To make the Bolognese sauce, heat the butter and 1 tbls olive oil over medium heat in a large frying pan. Add the onion and cook for 5 minutes or until soft but not browned, stirring occasionally.

2 Add the minced beef to the pan and mix with the onions, using a wooden spoon to break up the mince. Continue cooking for a further 5 minutes or until the meat is brown, stirring constantly. Stir in the dried mixed herbs, wine, tomato purée and salt and pepper to taste, then simmer gently, uncovered, for 15 minutes.

3 Meanwhile, cook the pasta. Bring a large saucepan of salted water to the boil, add the remaining oil and then the pasta. Return to the boil and cook for 8–10 minutes or until firm to the bite. To test the tagliatelle to see if it is ready, lift a piece out of the pan with a fork, leave to cool for a second or two, then bite into it. Carry on cooking for a minute or so if it's not yet done.

4 Drain the pasta thoroughly. Divide between individual serving dishes and pour on the sauce. Shave some Parmesan over each portion, if liked, and serve immediately, garnished with parsley.

BURGERS WITH SPICY BEAN SAUCE

SERVES 4
15 MINS TO PREPARE • 25 MINS TO COOK

450g/1lb minced
  beef
1 small onion, finely
  chopped
1 egg
1 tsp salt
1 tbls vegetable oil
1 garlic clove,
  crushed
1 red pepper, finely
  chopped
1 tsp ground cumin
400g/14oz tin baked
  beans
1 tbls tomato purée
50g/2oz Cheddar
  cheese, grated

NUTRITION NOTES

To cut down on the amount of fat in the burgers, use extra lean mince and grill the burgers rather than frying them. They will take about the same amount of time to cook but much of the fat from the meat will drip away.

1 Put the minced beef, half the onion, the egg and salt in a bowl and knead together with your fingers until the egg is absorbed.

2 Divide the mixture into four balls, then form each ball into a burger shape.

3 To make the sauce, heat the oil in a large frying pan. Add the remaining onion, the garlic and red pepper and fry over medium heat for 5 minutes or until soft, stirring frequently. Add the cumin and fry for a further 2 minutes, stirring. Add the baked beans and stir together well. Stir in the tomato purée, then leave the sauce to simmer for about 15 minutes or until thickened.

4 Meanwhile, cook the burgers: heat a large non-stick frying pan over medium heat. Add the burgers and fry for 5–6 minutes on each side or until they are done to your liking. Remove and drain on kitchen towels.

5 To serve, transfer the burgers to plates, top with the spicy bean sauce and sprinkle with grated cheese. Serve at once.

BEEF FAJITAS WITH HOT SALSA

SERVES 4
25 MINS TO PREPARE • 20 MINS TO COOK

500g/1lb 2oz
  beef steak (fillet)
9 tbls olive oil
75ml/3fl oz
  red wine
2 dried chillies,
  crushed
¼ tsp crushed black
  peppercorns
3 tbls fresh chopped
  chives
150ml/5fl oz
  soured cream
8 soft flour tortillas

FOR THE SALSA:
1 medium onion,
  peeled and finely
  chopped
2 garlic cloves,
  crushed and finely
  chopped
1 green pepper,
  de-seeded, pith
  removed and finely
  chopped
4 plum tomatoes,
  chopped
2 tbls Encona or
  similar chilli sauce

1 Cut the meat into thin strips along the grain, then place in a non-metallic dish. Sprinkle with 6 tbls of the oil, the wine, dried chillies and roughly crushed peppercorns. Leave to marinate at room temperature while you prepare the salsa.

2 To prepare the salsa, place the onion, garlic and green pepper in a colander or sieve and pour boiling water over them to soften them slightly. Whizz in a food processor or blender with the chopped plum tomatoes and chilli sauce.

3 In a small serving bowl, mix the chives with the soured cream and set aside.

4 Dry-fry the tortillas, or heat according to the manufacturer's instructions given on the packet. Keep warm until ready to use.

5 Put the remaining oil in a large, heavy-based frying pan or wok, lift the beef out of the marinade and stir-fry for about 2 minutes.

6 To serve, spread a tablespoonful of the soured cream mixture all over each tortilla, then top with a couple of spoonfuls of the stir-fried beef strips and carefully wrap the tortillas up to make fajitas. Serve the salsa separately as a topping or dipping sauce.

INGREDIENTS GUIDE

Tortillas are a cross between a bread and a pancake. Those made from corn may be deep-fried to make crisp shells or chips. Flour tortillas are best heated in a frying pan, without any oil, so that they remain soft enough to be rolled up.

GREEK LAMB MEATBALLS

MAKES ABOUT 20
15 MINS TO PREPARE • 15 MINS TO COOK

25ml/1fl oz milk
50g/2oz fresh
white breadcrumbs
350g/¾lb
minced lamb
½ onion,
finely chopped
2 tbls chopped
fresh parsley

1 tsp chopped
fresh mint,
or ½ tsp dried
1 egg, beaten
salt and pepper
25g/1oz flour
olive oil, for frying
mint leaves,
to garnish

1 Mix the milk and breadcrumbs in a bowl. Then, using your fingers, squeeze the milk from the breadcrumbs and pour off.

2 Add the lamb, onion, herbs and eggs to the bowl and mix well. Season to taste.

3 Break off a portion about the size of a walnut and roll it into a ball between the palms of your hands. Continue to make meatballs in this way until you have used up all the mince.

4 Sprinkle the flour on a plate, season and roll each meatball in it until evenly coated.

5 Pour the olive oil into a large frying pan to a depth of 12mm/½in and heat until very hot. Fry the meatballs, in batches if necessary, turning frequently until evenly browned.

6 As the meatballs cook, remove them from the pan with a slotted spoon and drain on absorbent paper. If serving hot, keep warm in a low oven; if serving cold, leave to cool then transfer to the fridge until ready to serve. Garnish with mint leaves to serve.

SERVING IDEAS

This recipe makes about 20 meatballs. To serve as part of a buffet dish for a party, double the quantities to make about 40 meatballs.

KOFTE WITH LEMON & CORIANDER SAUCE

SERVES 4 - 6
15 MINS TO PREPARE • 10 MINS TO COOK

2 eggs, beaten
900g/2lb lamb
 fillet, cubed
½ tsp ground
 coriander
½ tsp ground cumin
1 garlic clove,
 crushed
1 onion, roughly
 chopped
½ tsp salt
handful of fresh
 chopped coriander

FOR THE LEMON &
CORIANDER SAUCE:
4 egg yolks
4 tbls lemon juice
225ml/8fl oz water
25g/1oz fresh
 coriander leaves,
 chopped

1 Keeping the eggs aside, put all the remaining ingredients in a food processor or blender and mix to a smooth paste. Remove the paste from the blender and gradually mix in the beaten eggs. Knead the mixture with your hands until it is well blended and forms a pliable dough.

2 Dampen your hands so that the meat mixture doesn't stick to them, then break off egg-sized portions of the mixture and slip two portions on to each skewer.

3 Mould each portion of meat paste along the skewer to form a sausage shape. Heat the grill, and oil the grill pan. Place the kofte in the grill pan and cook for 10 minutes under high heat until well browned, turning the skewers frequently.

4 Meanwhile, make the sauce. Whisk the egg yolks in a heatproof bowl until pale and fluffy. Whisk in the lemon juice and water and blend well.

5 Place the bowl over a saucepan of gently simmering water and stir the mixture until it thickens, without boiling. Stir in the chopped coriander leaves and serve immediately with the kofte.

WHAT TO DRINK

Coriander is a difficult flavour to match with wine, but a dry red from Greece would fit the bill.

LAMB KEBABS WITH LEMON AND PARSLEY

MAKES 8 KEBABS
15 MINS TO PREPARE • 15 MINS TO COOK

900g/2lb boned lamb, cut into 2.5cm/1in cubes
8 small onions, quartered
16 bay leaves
oil for brushing

FOR THE MARINADE:
4 tbls lemon juice
4 garlic cloves, crushed
2 tbls chopped parsley

1 To make the marinade, mix together all the marinade ingredients in a bowl. Put the lamb pieces in the marinade, stir well and leave for 10 minutes or until ready to cook.

2 Lift the meat from the marinade. Thread the cubes of meat, the onion quarters and the bay leaves on to 8 skewers, then brush them with oil.

3 Place the kebabs under a hot grill and cook for 15 minutes, turning them and brushing them with more oil as needed. Serve at once, with salad and either pitta bread or rice.

LAMB CHOPS WITH WINE

SERVES 4
10 MINS TO PREPARE • 30 MINS TO COOK

8 x 150g/5oz lamb loin chops
salt and pepper
75g/3oz butter
2 tbls olive oil
4 tbls finely chopped onion
150ml/¼pt dry white wine
1 tbls finely chopped fresh tarragon or chives

2 tbls finely chopped parsley
4 tbls chicken stock

FOR THE GARNISH:
1 tsp finely chopped parsley
1 parsley sprig

1 Trim the chops, leaving a small border of fat around the meat. Wipe dry with kitchen towel, then season generously with pepper and salt.

2 Heat 25g/1oz butter and the oil in a frying pan large enough to take the chops in one layer. When the foaming subsides, lay the chops in the pan and brown them over medium heat for 3 mintues on each side. Turn down the heat and leave to cook for a further 7 minutes on each side. Remove the chops from the pan while you make the sauce.

3 To make the sauce, pour off and discard the fat from the frying pan and melt the remaining 50g/2oz butter. When it starts sizzling add the onion and cook for 2 minutes, stirring occasionally. Pour in the wine, chopped herbs and chicken stock and bring to the boil, scraping the brown crusty bits from the pan surface into the sauce. Boil rapidly for 5–6 minutes or until the sauce has thickened slightly.

4 Return the chops to the pan and bring the sauce back to a simmer.

5 Transfer the chops to a heated serving dish and pour the sauce over them. Sprinkle the remaining chopped parsley over the chops, garnish with the parsley sprig and serve at once.

MOROCCAN LAMB CHOPS

SERVES 4
10 MINS TO PREPARE • 15–25 MINS TO COOK

8 lamb loin chops
salt and pepper
flat-leaved parsley
and lemon wedges,
to garnish

FOR THE MARINADE:
4 tbls olive oil, plus
extra for greasing
2 tbls finely chopped
parsley

1 tbls lemon juice
½ tsp ground
cumin
¼-½ tsp cayenne
pepper
½ tsp finely crushed
black peppercorns
½ tsp ground
coriander
½ tsp ground
ginger

1 Trim the excess fat from the chops, leaving a narrow border; slash the fat at intervals with a sharp knife. Arrange the chops side by side in a dish just large enough to take them in a single layer.

2 Combine the marinade ingredients in a bowl, stirring until thoroughly mixed. Spread the marinade over both sides of the chops, cover and leave until ready to cook.

3 Heat the grill without the grid to high. Brush the grill grid with olive oil.

4 Remove the chops from the marinade and place them on the grid. Grill, 7.5cm/3in from the heat, until cooked to your taste (about 15 minutes for underdone, 20 minutes for medium or 25 minutes for well done). Turn them once while grilling, and brush occasionally with the marinade.

5 Arrange the grilled chops on a serving platter, season with salt and pepper and serve immediately, garnished with flat-leaved parsley and wedges of lemon.

SWEET & SOUR GRILLED SPARERIBS

SERVES 4
10 MINS TO PREPARE • 20 MINS TO COOK

900g/2lb pork
spareribs
1 tbls cornflour
lime wedges,
to serve (optional)

FOR THE SAUCE:
150ml/5fl oz
pineapple juice
75ml/3fl oz red
wine vinegar

1 tbls Worcestershire
sauce
2 tsp soy sauce
50g/2oz soft
brown sugar
5cm/2in piece fresh
root ginger,
chopped
1 garlic clove,
crushed
juice of 1 lime

1 Mix the sauce ingredients together in a jug and stir well. Brush some sauce over the ribs.

2 Heat the grill to medium and arrange the ribs on the grill pan. Grill for 15 minutes or until the ribs are well browned and cooked through. Turn them frequently to cook evenly on each side.

3 Mix the cornflour to a paste with a little water. Pour the reserved sauce into a small saucepan over medium heat and stir in the cornflour paste. Bring to the boil, then simmer for 3 minutes or until the sauce thickens. Serve with the ribs, garnished with lime wedges, if liked.

INGREDIENTS GUIDE

Sparerib of pork is different from spareribs. The spareribs used in this recipe are the long, thin ribs that are probably best known as a starter in Chinese cookery. These are taken from the belly of the pig. Sparerib of pork is a meatier cut of meat that is taken from the shoulder of the pig.

GREEN PEPPER & SHREDDED PORK

SERVES 4
15 MINS TO PREPARE • 5 MINS TO COOK

2 - 3 tbls dried black
  fungus ('wood ear')
200g/7oz pork fillet
½ tsp salt
1 tbls cornflour paste
  (made with ½ tbls
  water and ½ tbls
  cornflour)
3 tbls oil
½ tsp finely chopped
  fresh root ginger
1 tbls finely chopped
  spring onions, plus
  extra, to garnish
½ tsp finely chopped
  fresh garlic
1 tsp dried whole red
  chillies, soaked,
  de-seeded and
  chopped
100g/4oz green
  pepper, de-seeded
  and sliced
1 tsp sugar
1 tbls light soy sauce
2 tsp rice vinegar
1 - 2 tbls water

1 Soak the fungus (see Ingredients Guide), then rinse until the water runs clear. Drain well, then shred.

2 Cut the pork fillet into thin slices, put in a small bowl and mix with a pinch of the salt and half the cornflour paste.

3 Heat the oil in a pre-heated wok or large, heavy-based pan and add the pork. Stir-fry over medium heat for 1 minute or until the pork begins to change colour.

4 Add the ginger, garlic, spring onions and chilli. Stir-fry until they begin to release their aromas, then stir in the fungus and green pepper.

5 Add the remaining salt, the sugar, soy sauce, vinegar and water and continue stir-frying for 1 minute. Blend in the remaining cornflour paste and serve garnished with sliced spring onions.

INGREDIENTS GUIDE

Dried black fungus, also known as 'wood ear' or 'cloud ear', has a crunchy texture and a mild, subtle flavour. It is sold in polythene bags in Chinese and oriental food stores. Soak it in cold or warm water for 15 minutes (it will expand dramatically), then rinse in fresh cold water and drain well before use.

PORK IN A CREAMY PEPPERCORN SAUCE

SERVES 4
10 MINS TO PREPARE • 20 MINS TO COOK

50g/2oz butter
1 tbls olive oil
2 garlic cloves,
*   crushed*
4 boneless
*   pork chops*
2 tbls drained green
*   peppercorns in*
*   brine, lightly*
*   crushed*

1 Heat the butter and oil in a large frying pan over medium heat and add the garlic. Cook for 1 minute, stirring constantly, then add the pork chops and cook for a further 7 minutes on each side or until they are cooked through. Test with the tip of a knife to make sure the juices run clear, not pink. Remove the chops from the pan and keep warm.

2 Reduce the heat to low. Tip the frying pan to one side and spoon off all but 2 tbls of the juices, then add the peppercorns and chives.

3 Swirl in the crème fraîche and simmer for 2–3 minutes or until the sauce is thick and bubbling, stirring constantly. Add the brine and season with salt and pepper to taste. Pour over the pork chops and serve at once.

PORK CHOPS WITH CIDER SAUCE

SERVES 4
5 MINS TO PREPARE • 25 MINS TO COOK

1 tbls olive oil
4 pork chops
25g/1oz butter
½ onion,
*   thinly sliced*
10 - 12 juniper
*   berries*

1 crisp dessert apple
1 tsp flour
200ml/7fl oz
*   dry cider*
salt and pepper

1 Heat the oil in a large frying pan. Seal the chops by frying over high heat for 2 minutes on each side. Lower the heat to medium and continue cooking for a further 4 minutes on each side or until they are cooked through: test with the tip of a knife to make sure the juices run clear, not pink, then remove from the pan and keep warm.

2 To make the sauce, add the butter to the frying pan and melt over a medium heat. When hot, add the onion and juniper berries and fry for 5 minutes or until the onion begins to brown, stirring frequently. Quarter and core the apple and cut into 3mm/⅛in slices. Add to the pan and fry for 2–3 minutes or until the apple begins to brown slightly, stirring often.

3 Sprinkle the flour over the apple and onion and cook for 2 minutes, stirring. Pour in the cider, stirring constantly. Bring to the boil and simmer for 3 minutes, stirring occasionally, or until thickened. The apple should be soft but still retain its shape. Season to taste and return the chops to the pan for 2–3 minutes to heat them through. Serve immediately.

INGREDIENTS GUIDE

The strong, slightly woody taste of juniper berries mixes well with the sweetness of apple and cider in this dish. The berries, which are sold dried, can be used whole or crushed lightly in food: they are often used to flavour rich meats, such as venison and wood pigeon, or jellies and pickles. Store juniper berries in an airtight container.

HEARTY LEEK BROTH

SERVES 6
15 MINS TO PREPARE • 15 MINS TO COOK

350g/12oz piece of smoked bacon
450g/1lb leeks
350g/12oz new potatoes, scrubbed and cut into quarters
2 carrots, sliced
1 parsnip, cut into 12mm/½in chunks

175g/6oz swede, cut into 12mm/½in chunks
1 tbls fine oatmeal
25g/1oz butter
2-3 sprigs fresh thyme
1.7L/3pt chicken or vegetable stock
salt and pepper

1 Cut the bacon into 20mm/¾in cubes, discarding any rind.

2 Clean the leeks, then cut into 12mm/½in-thick slices, including some of the green part.

3 Put the potatoes, carrots, parsnip and swede into a large bowl. Add the leeks. Sprinkle with oatmeal and toss until the vegetables are coated.

4 Melt the butter in a large saucepan and add the cubes of bacon. Fry gently over medium heat for 3–4 minutes until lightly browned, stirring frequently. Add all the vegetables and the sprigs of fresh thyme, cover and cook over low heat for a further 3–4 minutes until slightly softened.

5 Pour in the stock and season to taste with salt and pepper. Bring to the boil, then partly cover and leave to simmer gently for 15 minutes. Check from time to time and use a slotted spoon to remove any scum that may have risen to the surface.

6 Adjust the seasoning just before serving.

BANGERS WITH ONION GRAVY

SERVES 4
15 MINS TO PREPARE • 25 MINS TO COOK

8 good-quality sausages
1-2 tbls vegetable oil
700g/1½lb onions, thinly sliced
pinch of sugar
2 tsp flour

500ml/18fl oz beef stock
1 tsp Worcestershire sauce
salt and pepper
chopped parsley, to garnish (optional)

1 Grill the sausages under medium heat for 10–15 minutes or until they are well browned and cooked through, turning often.

2 Meanwhile heat the oil in a large frying pan. Add the onions and sugar and stir well. Reduce the heat to low and cook for 15 minutes, stirring occasionally, until the onions are very soft and lightly browned.

3 Stir in the flour and cook for 2 minutes, stirring constantly. Add the stock and Worcestershire sauce and continue cooking for 5 minutes or until the gravy is slightly reduced and thickened, stirring often.

4 Add the sausages to the pan, increase the heat to medium and cook for 5 minutes or until heated through, turning often. Season to taste, transfer to a serving dish and sprinkle with parsley, if liked.

SAUSAGE & CHICKEN JAMBALAYA

SERVES 4
20 MINS TO PREPARE • 20 MINS TO COOK

225g/½lb spicy sausage, sliced
2 skinless, boneless chicken breasts
1 large onion
3 garlic cloves
4 celery sticks
2 green peppers, de-seeded
2 tbls olive oil
575ml/1pt chicken stock
350g/12oz long-grain rice
2 tsp chopped fresh thyme or 1 tsp dried
½ - 1 tsp cayenne pepper
salt

1 With a sharp knife, cut the sausage into thick slices and the chicken into bite-sized pieces. Finely chop the onion, crush the garlic, slice the celery and chop the peppers.

2 Heat the oil over medium heat in a large, heavy-based frying pan or sauté pan with a lid. Add the sausage and the chicken and fry for about 5 minutes or until cooked through, stirring occasionally. Add the onion, celery, green pepper and garlic and fry for a further minute, stirring often.

3 Pour in the stock, then stir in the rice, thyme and cayenne pepper. Bring to the boil, then reduce the heat, cover the pan and leave to simmer for about 12 minutes.

4 Remove the lid and check the rice to see if it is cooked; if not, check again after a few minutes. As soon as the rice is tender, stir the jambalaya, season with salt to taste and serve.

INGREDIENTS GUIDE

In America, Chicken & Sausage Jambalaya is usually made with a spicy smoked pork sausage called andouille. In this recipe, we have used kabanos, a similar smoky-flavoured sausage from Poland. Other highly seasoned sausages that you can use include chorizo, a Spanish pork sausage flavoured with paprika, and kielbasa, a Polish smoked sausage made with pork and beef.

MUSHROOM
& BACON RICE

SERVES 4
10 MINS TO PREPARE • 25 MINS TO COOK

**700ml/25fl oz
chicken stock
350g/12oz
'easy cook'
long-grain rice
1 tbls olive oil
1 onion, chopped
350g/12oz streaky
bacon, cut into
strips**

**2 tsp chopped
fresh thyme
or 1 tsp dried
350g/12oz
mushrooms, sliced
chopped parsley,
to garnish**

1 Put the stock in a large saucepan over medium heat and bring to the boil. Reduce the heat to low and add the rice to the pan. Simmer for 20 minutes or until the rice is cooked. It should be firm, but not crunchy, when you bite into it.

2 Meanwhile, heat the oil in a large frying pan or sauté pan over medium heat and fry the onion and bacon for 5 minutes, stirring now and then. Add the thyme and mushrooms and cook for a further 5 minutes, stirring.

3 Tip the rice into the pan and mix well with the cooked vegetables. Continue cooking for a further 5 minutes or until the rice is heated through, stirring. Serve at once, with the chopped parsley sprinkled over the top.

GOLDEN PASTA GRILL

SERVES 4 • 25 MINS TO PREPARE • 20 MINS TO COOK

**salt and pepper
2 tbls olive oil
350g/12oz
dried penne
100g/4oz button
mushrooms, sliced
50g/2oz smoked
streaky bacon,
cut into strips
1 red pepper,
de-seeded and
thinly sliced**

**2 courgettes, chopped
25g/1oz butter
25g/1oz flour
275ml/½pt milk
150g/5oz mature
Cheddar cheese,
grated
50g/2oz frozen peas
snipped chives, to
garnish (optional)
2 tbls snipped fresh
chives, optional**

1 Bring a large pan of salted water to the boil and add 1 tbls olive oil. Add the penne and cook for 10–12 minutes or until just tender.

2 Meanwhile, heat the remaining oil in a frying pan. Add the mushrooms, bacon, red pepper and courgettes and cook over low heat for 10 minutes or until the vegetables are tender, stirring frequently.

3 To make the sauce, melt the butter and add the flour, stirring constantly over low heat for 3 minutes. Increase the heat to medium and gradually blend in the milk, stirring constantly until the sauce boils and thickens. Simmer over very low heat for 2 minutes, stir in 75g/3oz cheese, the frozen peas and salt and pepper to taste. Cook for a further minute.

4 Mix the cooked, drained pasta and the cooked vegetable and bacon mixture into the sauce and transfer to a heatproof serving dish. Sprinkle with the remaining grated cheese and place under a hot grill until the cheese is golden and bubbling. Garnish with the chives, if liked, and serve hot.

TAGLIATELLE WITH LEEK & MUSHROOM SAUCE

SERVES 4
10 MINS TO PREPARE • 15 MINS TO COOK

*350g/12oz green
  tagliatelle*
2 tbls olive oil

FOR THE SAUCE:
25g/1oz butter
2 leeks, sliced
*175g/6oz button
  mushrooms, halved*

*225g/6oz ham,
  sliced into strips*
*100g/4oz
  frozen peas*
2 tsp flour
*275ml/½pt
  soured cream*
*chopped flat-leaved
  parsley, to garnish*

1 Bring a large saucepan of water to the boil, add the pasta and simmer until just soft. Drain and stir in 1 tbls of the olive oil.

2 Melt the butter in a large heavy-based saucepan and add the leeks with the remaining olive oil. Fry over medium heat until the leeks are soft but not brown, stirring frequently. Add the mushrooms and ham and cook for a further 3 minutes, stirring constantly.

3 Stir in the frozen peas and cook until they have de-frosted, stirring constantly.

4 Sprinkle in the flour and stir in the soured cream. Stir constantly over medium heat until the cream has thickened and thoroughly heated through.

5 Put the pasta in a warmed serving dish and pour the sauce over it. Garnish with chopped flat-leaved parsley before serving.

THREE-COLOUR PASTA SALAD

SERVES 4
20 MINS TO PREPARE • 15 MINS TO COOK

*175g/6oz mixed
  tomato, spinach
  and egg dried
  pasta spirals
  (fusilli tricolori)*
*50g/2oz frozen
  petits pois, cooked
  and cooled*
*half a 198g/6½oz
  tin sweetcorn,
  drained*
*100g/4oz cherry
  tomatoes, halved*
*6 spring onions,
  trimmed and
  chopped*
*½ small red pepper,
  de-seeded and
  finely chopped*

*100g/4oz cooked
  chicken, cut
  into strips*
*100g/4oz cooked
  ham, cut into strips*

**FOR THE
LEMON DRESSING:**
*125ml/4fl oz
  sunflower oil*
juice of a lemon
*2 garlic cloves,
  crushed*
4 tsp French mustard
*salt and freshly
  ground black
  pepper*
*4 tsp chopped
  fresh parsley*

1 Cook the pasta in a large saucepan of boiling salted water for 9–12 minutes or according to the instructions on the packet.

2 Meanwhile, put all the ingredients for the lemon dressing in a bowl and beat together well. Drain the pasta thoroughly, and put it in a large serving bowl. While the pasta is still warm, stir in the lemon dressing.

3 Add the petits pois, sweetcorn, tomatoes, onion and red pepper.

4 Stir in the strips of chicken and ham and season with salt and pepper to taste.

CHILLI CHICKEN LIVERS

SERVES 4
20 MINS TO PREPARE • 25 MINS TO COOK

450g/1lb chicken livers
1 tbls olive oil
1 onion, chopped
2 garlic cloves, crushed
400g/14oz tin chopped tomatoes
1 tbls tomato purée

1 tsp dried mixed herbs
¼ tsp chilli powder
1 tbls flour
25g/1oz butter
100g/4oz
   button mushrooms, sliced
150ml/5fl oz red wine

1 Cut the chicken livers into slices and pat dry with kitchen towels.

2 Heat the oil in a saucepan over medium heat and add the onion and garlic. Fry for 5 minutes or until the onions are translucent but not brown, stirring frequently. Add the tomatoes, then bring to the boil and simmer for 5 minutes.

3 Stir in the tomato purée, herbs and chilli powder and simmer, uncovered, for 10 minutes or so until the sauce thickens.

4 Meanwhile, put the flour in a bowl and turn the chicken livers in it until completely coated. Melt the butter in a large frying pan and add the floured liver. Fry for 5 minutes or until the liver is lightly browned, stirring constantly.

5 Add the mushrooms to the livers and fry for a further 3 minutes, stirring. Add the tomato sauce to the pan, stir in the wine and bring to the boil. Lower the heat and simmer for 5–7 minutes or until the livers are cooked through. Serve at once.

INGREDIENTS GUIDE

If you are using frozen chicken livers, thaw them thoroughly before use, then drain and dry them on kitchen towels. Though frozen chicken livers are more convenient, fresh are preferable; they are firmer and have a better texture.

STIR-FRIED LIVER

SERVES 4
20 MINS TO PREPARE • 5 MINS TO COOK

450g/1lb pig's liver, in one piece
1 tbls cornflour
1 tsp salt
1 tsp ground ginger
1 tbls medium-dry sherry
5 tbls oil
1½ tbls coarsely chopped spring onion tops

1 large garlic clove, crushed

FOR THE SAUCE:
1½ tbls soy sauce
1 tbls medium-dry sherry
1 tbls tomato purée
1½ tbls chicken stock
1 tsp sugar

1 Trim away all traces of thin outer skin or veins from the liver. Using a sharp knife, cut into 3mm/⅛in thick slices, then into 2.5cm/1in strips.

2 Put the cornflour in a bowl and mix with the salt and ginger. Stir in 2tbls water, the sherry and 1 tbls oil. Mix until smooth.

3 Add the liver slices and gently turn to coat with the cornflour mixture. Leave to stand for 15 minutes.

4 Put all the sauce ingredients into a mixing bowl and stir until well blended.

5 Heat the remaining oil in a frying pan over medium heat. When it sizzles, add the liver, spreading the pieces evenly over the pan. Increase the heat and cook briskly, stirring, for 30 seconds.

6 Sprinkle in the garlic and spring onion and continue stir-frying for another 30 seconds. Pour the sauce mixture into the pan, bring to the boil and cook, stirring constantly, for a further 30 seconds. Serve hot with boiled rice.

VENETIAN LIVER WITH ONIONS & SAGE

SERVES 4
15 MINS TO PREPARE • 20 MINS TO COOK

3 tbls olive oil
275g/10oz onion, thinly sliced
1 tsp chopped fresh sage
700g/1½lb calf's liver, thinly sliced

salt and pepper
3 tbls white wine vinegar
2 tbls finely chopped parsley
sage sprigs, to garnish (optional)

1 Cut the liver crossways into strips and wipe dry with kitchen towels. Season with salt and pepper to taste.

2 Heat 2 tbls oil in a large frying pan over medium heat. Add the onions and cook for 8 minutes or until very soft, stirring frequently. Add the chopped sage and continue to cook for 2 minutes, stirring often. When the onions begin to colour, remove the pan from the heat.

3 Heat the remaining oil in another frying pan over medium heat and add the liver strips. Cook for 3 minutes or until they are no longer red, turning frequently. Add the onions and continue to cook for 2 minutes or until heated through. Transfer to a warmed serving dish.

4 Put the pan in which the liver was cooked over a medium heat and add the vinegar. Scrape the bottom of the pan with a wooden spatula to incorporate any crusty bits and cook, stirring constantly, for 2–3 minutes or until reduced to about 2 tbls. Pour this over the liver and onions and serve immediately, sprinkled with the parsley. Garnish with fresh sage, if liked.

LIVER WITH ORANGE SAUCE

SERVES 4
15 MINS TO PREPARE • 25 MINS TO COOK

**700g/1½lb
  lamb's liver
50g/2oz shallots
50g/2oz butter
25g/1oz plain flour
275ml/½pt
  brown stock
zest and juice of
  one orange**

**150ml/5fl oz
  red wine
1 tbls redcurrant jelly
1 tbls oil
orange slices,
  to garnish**

1 Finely chop the shallots. Heat 25g/1oz of the butter in a small, heavy saucepan. Add the shallots and fry gently for about 5 minutes. Stir in the flour and continue stirring for 2–3 minutes. Pour in the brown stock. Stir vigorously when mixing in the stock to break up any lumps. Bring to the boil, stirring continuously until the sauce has thickened.

2 Cut the orange zest into 3mm/¼in wide strips and add to the sauce, together with the orange juice and the red wine. Bring to the boil and simmer gently until reduced by half, then stir in the redcurrant jelly.

3 Meanwhile, wash the liver and pat it dry on kitchen towels. Heat the remaining butter and the oil in a griddle pan. Add the liver, reduce the heat and fry for about 5 minutes on each side. Cut the liver into thin slices and arrange in fans on a warmed serving dish.

4 Return the sauce to the boil, then pour a little over the liver and garnish with slices of orange. Serve immediately with the remaining sauce in a separate sauce boat.

WHAT TO DRINK

A fruity, crisp red wine with a brush of acidity would be good with this dish. Try an Italian Montepulciano d'Abruzzo.

THAI-STYLE RICE NOODLES WITH CHICKEN

SERVES 4
20 MINS TO PREPARE • 25 MINS TO COOK

300g/11oz chicken breast, cut into strips
juice and zest of 1 lime
1 tbls light soy sauce
2 pieces of lemon grass
200ml/7fl oz coconut milk
75g/3oz thin dried rice noodles
2 tbls vegetable oil
2 garlic cloves, crushed
5cm/2in long piece of galangal, peeled and sliced
1 small red (bird's eye) chilli, chopped
1 small green (bird's eye) chilli, chopped
175g/6oz mushrooms, sliced
3 lime leaves, shredded
150g/5oz bean shoots
10g/¼oz fresh coriander leaves, chopped

1 Put the chicken in a dish, add the lime juice and soy sauce and marinate for 10 minutes.

2 Roughly chop the lemon grass and place in a small pan with the coconut milk. Put the pan over low heat and bring to the boil. Remove from the heat and leave to infuse for 5 minutes. Strain and reserve the flavoured coconut milk.

3 Place the noodles in a large bowl and cover with plenty of boiling water. Leave to soak for 5 minutes, then drain.

4 Heat the oil in a large frying pan over high heat. Add the garlic, galangal and red and green chillies, fry briefly, then lower the heat and add the mushrooms and the chicken plus marinade.

5 Cook until the chicken is white all over, then add the flavoured coconut milk and lime leaves.

6 Stir in the bean shoots and simmer gently for 5 minutes. Stir in the rice noodles and chopped coriander. Sprinkle with the lime zest and serve immediately.

INGREDIENTS GUIDE

Galangal is a root that closely resembles ginger in both appearance and taste. Use it in any dish that would normally call for fresh root ginger. Lemon grass also has a tinge of ginger about it, but the predominant flavours are citrus and grass! Bird's eye chillies are very tiny, extremely hot chillies from Thailand. Use a milder chilli if you do not like your food too spicy hot.

You can buy galangal, bird's eye chillies and lemon grass in most supermarkets or oriental food stores.

THAI RED CHICKEN CURRY

SERVES 4 - 6
15 MINS TO PREPARE • 10 MINS TO COOK

*450g/1lb chicken
thigh meat
225g/½lb tin bamboo
shoots, drained
1 small onion
1 garlic clove
25mm/1in fresh
root ginger or
galangal
2 tbls vegetable oil*

*1 tbls lime
or lemon juice
2 tbls fish sauce
2 tbls Thai red
curry paste
275ml/½pt
coconut milk
1 tsp salt
fresh coriander
leaves, to garnish*

1 Cut the chicken meat into thin strips. Thinly shred the bamboo shoots. Finely chop the onion and garlic. Peel the root ginger or galangal and cut it into fine shreds.

2 In a preheated wok or large frying pan, heat the oil until it is very hot but not smoking. Add the chicken, onion, garlic and ginger or galangal and stir-fry for 3–4 minutes or until lightly browned.

3 Stir in the lime or lemon juice, fish sauce, curry paste and coconut milk. Bring to the boil and cook for 2–3 minutes, stirring constantly.

4 Add the bamboo shoots and salt. Continue cooking for a further 2–3 minutes. Garnish with chopped and whole coriander leaves and serve immediately.

INGREDIENTS GUIDE

Don't confuse the coconut milk used in this recipe with the juice found in a coconut – the milk is made by steeping coconut flesh in hot water. Many supermarkets and specialist stores sell tinned coconut milk, which is by far the easiest to use, but you can also buy blocks of compressed creamed coconut that are reconstituted by dissolving in boiling water – just follow the instructions on the packet.

Thai red curry paste has become increasingly available and can now be found in many supermarkets. In Thailand, curry pastes are prepared with fresh rather than dried ingredients, but shop-bought pastes are a convenient substitute. There are two different curry pastes used in Thai cooking – green and red. Red is the milder of the two.

CHICKEN FU-YUNG
(LOTUS WHITE CHICKEN)

SERVES 4
20 MINS TO PREPARE • 10 MINS TO COOK

2 chicken breast
fillets (approx
250g/9oz), skinned
1 tsp salt
1 tsp Chinese rice
wine
½ tsp finely chopped
fresh root ginger
1 tbls cornflour paste
(made with ½ tbls
water and ½ tbls
cornflour)

4 egg whites,
lightly beaten
2 tbls milk
oil for deep-frying
1 tbls finely chopped
spring onions
1 small lettuce heart,
shredded
50g/2oz mangetout
4 tbls chicken stock
½ tsp sesame oil

1 Cut the chicken breasts into thin slices, then put them in a bowl with a pinch of the salt, the rice wine, ginger, cornflour paste, egg whites and milk. Blend well.

2 Heat the oil until medium-hot in a pre-heated wok or large, heavy-based frying pan. Drain the chicken slices and add them to the wok. Deep-fry for 30–45 seconds only. Remove them from the oil using a straining spoon, and leave to drain on kitchen towel.

3 Pour the excess oil out of the pan, leaving about 1 tbls. Add the spring onions, lettuce and mangetout and stir-fry for 1–2 minutes. Add the remaining salt and the stock and bring to the boil. When the stock is boiling, return the chicken to the pan and braise for about 1 minute. Sprinkle with sesame oil and serve immediately.

COOK'S TIPS

In Chinese cooking, most vegetables are cut into small pieces so that they can be quickly stir-fried, so retaining their flavour, crunchiness and essential nutrients. When shredding vegetables it is easiest to use a large cleaver — but be careful how you handle it. Cut the vegetable into uniform slices about 3–6mm/⅛–¼in wide, then cut across the slices to form shreds.

ASIAN FRIED RICE

SERVES 4 - 6
10 MINS TO PREPARE • 10 MINS TO COOK

2 eggs, lightly beaten
salt and pepper
4 tbls vegetable oil
4 shallots, peeled and
  thinly sliced or
  chopped
1 garlic clove, finely
  chopped
½ tsp shrimp paste
1 tbls light soy sauce
1 tbls tomato purée
450g/1lb cooked
  long grain rice,
  cooled

225g/½lb cooked
  meat (beef, lamb,
  chicken or pork),
  chopped

TO GARNISH:
100g/4oz cooked
  peeled tiger
  prawns
fresh coriander
  leaves

1 Heat 3 tbls oil in a wok or large frying pan and lightly brown the shallots and garlic. Add the shrimp paste, soy sauce and tomato purée and stir-fry for about 2 minutes.

2 Stir the cold cooked rice and meat into the pan. Cook for 4–5 minutes until warmed through, stirring constantly.

3 Meanwhile season the beaten eggs with salt and pepper and make an omelette, frying it in the remaining oil. Turn the omelette on to a chopping board and cut into thin strips.

4 Transfer the fried rice mixture to a warm serving dish or platter and garnish with the omelette strips, cooked peeled prawns and coriander leaves. Serve hot.

CHICKEN & CASHEW NUTS

SERVES 4
20 MINS TO PREPARE • 10 MINS TO COOK

4 skinless, boneless chicken breasts
1 egg white
1 tsp cornflour
1 tsp soy sauce
1 tsp dry sherry
1 clove garlic
25mm/1in cube fresh root ginger
4 spring onions
1 large carrot
2 tbls peanut or vegetable oil
75g/3oz salted cashew nuts
2 tbls hoisin sauce

1 Cut the chicken breast into strips. In a non-metallic bowl, mix the egg white with the cornflour, soy sauce and sherry. Add the chicken and mix well to coat thoroughly.

2 Finely chop the garlic and peel and finely chop the ginger. Cut the spring onions into pieces 25mm/1in long and the carrot into thin strips. Heat a wok or large frying pan and add the oil. When it is hot, add the garlic and ginger and stir. Add the spring onions and carrot and stir-fry for 1 minute. Remove from the pan with a slotted spoon and keep warm.

3 Add the chicken and stir-fry for 2–3 minutes. Return the vegetables to the wok.

4 Add the cashew nuts and hoisin sauce to the wok and stir-fry for a further minute or until the chicken is cooked through and the nuts and sauce are blended in. Serve at once.

INGREDIENTS GUIDE

Hoisin sauce is a Chinese barbecue sauce. It is available ready-made from supermarkets but it's easy to make your own version.

For the above recipe simply mix 1 tbls soy sauce, 1 tbls dry sherry and 1 tbls dark brown sugar and use instead of the 2 tbls hoisin sauce.

HOT CHICKEN SALAD

SERVES 4
10 MINS TO PREPARE
5 MINS TO COOK

**2 large chicken breasts,
  skinned and boned**
2 tbls harissa paste
**½ a large iceberg or
  pale cos lettuce**
**100g/4oz red cherry
  tomatoes**
1 yellow pepper, finely sliced
1 tbls sunflower oil
**50g/2oz flaked almonds,
  lightly toasted**

FOR THE DRESSING:
275ml/½pt plain yogurt
4 tbls olive oil
2 tbls lemon juice
2 garlic cloves, crushed
1 tsp mustard
1 tbls finely chopped mint
1 tsp sugar
**salt and freshly ground
  black pepper**

INGREDIENTS GUIDE

Harissa paste is a smooth red sauce made of chilli peppers which is very hot and spicy. It is a speciality of Tunisia and can be bought in delicatessens and some large supermarkets.

1 Finely slice the chicken breasts, then put them in a bowl and add the harissa paste. Leave to marinate at room temperature until you are ready to cook them.

2 Wash and dry the lettuce and tear it into small pieces. Halve the tomatoes and put them in a bowl with the lettuce and pepper. Mix lightly, ensuring that the vegetables don't drop to the bottom.

3 Combine all the ingredients for the dressing in a small bowl, beating to mix thoroughly, or put them in a screwtop jar, fit the lid and then shake the jar to blend.

4 Put a heavy-based frying pan or wok over high heat. When the pan is really hot, add the sunflower oil and continue to heat until it starts to smoke. Toss in the sliced chicken with the marinade, then stir-fry until the flesh is firm and cooked through.

5 Lift the chicken out of the pan and arrange on top of the salad. Sprinkle with the flaked almonds. Remove the garlic cloves from the dressing, then pour the dressing over the salad and serve immediately.

CLASSIC CORONATION CHICKEN

SERVES 4 - 6
20 MINS TO PREPARE • 15 MINS TO COOK

25g/1oz butter
1 onion, finely
  chopped
1 garlic clove,
  crushed
2.5cm/2in cube of
  fresh root ginger,
  finely chopped
1 tsp ground cumin
1 tsp ground
  coriander
½ tsp turmeric
½ tsp chilli powder
1 tbls tomato purée
3 tbls hot mango
  chutney
150ml/5fl oz
  pineapple juice

juice and zest of
  1 lime
225ml/8fl oz
  mayonnaise
3 tbls Greek-style
  yogurt
salt and freshly
  ground black
  pepper
3 tbls fresh chopped
  coriander
5 thin slices of
  pineapple
1 cooked chicken,
  skin and bones
  removed
shredded lettuce
  leaves, to serve

1 Melt the butter in a heavy-based frying pan. Add the onion, garlic and ginger. Fry over low heat until the onion is just soft.

2 Add the cumin, ground coriander, turmeric and chilli powder and cook for a few seconds, then add the tomato purée, mango chutney and pineapple juice. Simmer over low heat for 5 minutes, stirring occasionally.

3 Remove the pan from the heat and pour the sauce through a sieve into a bowl. Stir in the lime juice and zest, then leave to cool.

4 When the sauce has cooled, whisk in the mayonnaise and yogurt and season to taste with salt and freshly ground black pepper. Stir in the fresh chopped coriander.

5 Cut 3 of the pineapple slices into segments, then fold them into the sauce. Cut the cooked chicken into bite-sized pieces and stir them into the sauce as well.

6 Cut the remaining pineapple slices in half. Spoon the mixture on to a bed of shredded lettuce leaves and garnish with the pineapple slices.

CREAMY CHICKEN & ALMONDS

SERVES 4
10 MINS TO PREPARE • 25 MINS TO COOK

600g/1¼lb skinless,
  boneless chicken
  breasts
salt and pepper
50g/2oz butter
2 tbls olive oil
1 large Spanish
  onion, chopped
1 garlic clove,
  finely chopped

4 tbls Madeira
juice of ½ lemon
275ml/½pt double
  cream
4 tbls flaked
  almonds, lightly
  toasted
lemon slices,
  to garnish

1 Cut the chicken breasts diagonally across the grain into slices about 6mm/¼in thick. Season generously with salt and pepper.

2 Heat the butter and oil in a large frying pan over medium heat. Add the onion and garlic and cook for 5 minutes or until soft but not coloured, stirring frequently.

3 Add the chicken slices and fry for 5 minutes or until cooked through, stirring constantly. Add the Madeira and cook over high heat for 10 minutes or until the Madeira and the cooking juices have reduced to half their original quantity, stirring constantly.

4 Reduce the heat to low, stir in the lemon juice, then stir in the cream. Cook for a few minutes or until the sauce has heated through. Scatter with the almonds, garnish with lemon slices and serve at once.

DEVILLED DRUMSTICKS

SERVES 8
15 MINS TO PREPARE • 25 MINS TO COOK

16 small chicken drumsticks
6 tbls oil
1 large onion, finely chopped
6 tbls lemon juice
6 tbls soy sauce
½ tsp salt
pinch black pepper
2 tsp ground coriander
4 tbls soft brown sugar
4 tbls plum jam
lime slices and celery leaves, to garnish

1 Make 2–3 slashes in each drumstick with a sharp knife. Mix together all the remaining ingredients except the onion and 3 tbls oil.

2 Heat the 3 tbls oil in a heavy based frying pan over medium heat and add the chopped onion. Cook over medium heat for 2–3 minutes until transparent. Add the drumsticks and continue to cook for five minutes or until browned on each side. Pour the sugar and soy sauce mixture over the drumsticks. Continue cooking for 15–20 minutes, stirring occasionally, until the chicken is cooked.

3 Put the drumsticks on a serving plate, garnish with lime slices and celery leaves and serve.

SERVING IDEAS

This dish is ideal for picnics and the sweetness makes it popular with children.

The drumsticks will come to no harm if the serving dish is covered with foil and put in a low oven to keep warm for 30 minutes or so.

CHICKEN BLANQUETTE

SERVES 4
15 MINS TO PREPARE • 20 MINS TO COOK

**1.4-1.6kg/3-3½lb
  cooked chicken
50g/2oz butter
100g/4oz button
  mushrooms, halved
juice of ½ lemon
15g/½oz flour
salt and pepper**

**600ml/1pt chicken
  stock
150ml/¼pt double
  cream
2 egg yolks
chervil sprigs and
  lemon wedges,
  to garnish**

1 Melt 25g/1oz of the butter in a small saucepan, add the mushrooms and lemon juice and simmer for 5 minutes. Remove the mushrooms with a slotted spoon and keep warm.

2 To make the sauce, melt the remaining butter in a saucepan and stir in the flour. Stir for 2–3 minutes until the mixture is smooth but has not changed colour. Stir in the chicken stock a little at a time. Bring to the boil, season to taste and simmer very gently for 5 minutes.

3 Mix the cream and egg yolks together in a bowl and pour in a little of the sauce, stirring constantly. Return to the rest of the sauce, stirring well. Heat gently, stirring constantly, until the sauce thickens; do not boil. Add the mushrooms and correct the seasoning.

4 To serve, divide the chicken into eight pieces (remove the skin if you wish). Arrange on a heated serving dish and spoon the sauce over the top. Garnish and serve hot.

TURKEY PAPRIKA IN SOURED CREAM

SERVES 4
15 MINS TO PREPARE • 25 MINS TO COOK

**50g/2oz butter
450g/1lb turkey
  escalopes
2 onions, chopped
2 green peppers,
  thinly sliced**

**1 tbls paprika
1 tbls flour
275ml/½pt
  soured cream**

1 Melt the butter over low heat in a large saucepan or sauté pan that has a close-fitting lid. Add the turkey and fry briefly, just until lightly browned on each side. Do this in batches, if necessary.

2 Using a slotted spoon, remove the turkey from the pan and set aside. Add the peppers and onions to the fat remaining in the pan and fry for 5 minutes or until soft, stirring often. Sprinkle on the paprika and cook for 2 minutes, stirring constantly.

3 Return the turkey to the pan and cover. Cook for 10 minutes or until the turkey is tender, turning over halfway through. With a slotted spoon, remove the turkey and keep warm.

4 Sprinkle the flour into the pan and continue cooking for 3 minutes, stirring constantly. Stir in the soured cream and cook for a further 5 minutes or until the cream is heated through and the sauce has thickened. Pour the sauce over the turkey to serve.

TURKEY BALTI CURRY

SERVES 4
15 MINS TO PREPARE • 25 MINS TO COOK

4 tbls olive oil
4 garlic cloves,
  crushed and finely
  chopped
2.5cm/1in cube of
  fresh root ginger,
  finely chopped
4 shallots, roughly
  chopped
450g/1lb turkey
  breast, cut into
  strips
4 dried red chillies,
  de-seeded and
  crushed
4 medium tomatoes,
  quartered
1 yellow pepper, cut
  into 1cm/½in cubes
4 tbls passata
3 tbls fresh coriander
  leaves, chopped,
  plus extra to
  garnish

FOR THE
BALTI SPICE MIX:
2 tbls coriander seeds
1 tbls cumin seeds
½ tbls fennel seeds
seeds of 12
  cardamom pods
5cm/2in-long piece
  of cinnamon stick
2 bay leaves, torn
  into small shreds
4 cloves
a little grated nutmeg
2 tsp mild curry
  powder
½ tsp chilli powder

1 First prepare the Balti spice mix. Heat a Balti pan, heavy-based frying pan or wok, then dry-fry the coriander seeds over high heat for about 30 seconds. Add the cumin and fennel seeds, the cardamom seeds, cinnamon stick and bay leaves and fry for a further minute or so, stirring constantly. Tip the spices into a bowl when they are brown but not burned. Break up the cinnamon stick and pound to a powder, then stir in the remaining spice mix ingredients.

2 Heat the oil in the frying pan and stir in the garlic and ginger. Cook for 2 minutes, then add the shallots. Fry for 5 minutes or until soft. Stir in the spice mixture and cook for a further 2 minutes.

3 Add the turkey to the pan and stir-fry for 5 minutes or until all surfaces of the meat are sealed.

4 Add 3 tbls water to prevent sticking, then add the chillies, tomatoes, yellow pepper and passata and stir-fry for 5 minutes or until the turkey is cooked.

5 Add the chopped coriander leaves, stir-fry for 1 minute, then serve on a bed of rice and garnish with a few whole, fresh coriander leaves.

CHUNKY TURKEY BURGERS

SERVES 4
15 MINS TO PREPARE • 10 MINS TO COOK

450g/1lb turkey
  escalopes
½ an onion, peeled
1 tsp dried thyme
2 tbls tomato ketchup
salt and freshly
  ground black pepper

2 tbls flour
1 egg, beaten
75g/3oz fresh
  breadcrumbs
2 tbls sesame seeds
vegetable oil for
  shallow frying

1 Chop the turkey escalopes finely and put them in a bowl. Chop the onion finely and add it to the turkey meat. Add the thyme and tomato ketchup and season to taste with salt and freshly ground black pepper. Mix thoroughly.

2 Form the mixture into four large burgers in your hands. Spread the flour on a plate and turn each burger in the flour, then dip them in the beaten egg.

3 Mix the breadcrumbs with the sesame seeds and place them in a shallow dish. Coat the burgers with the breadcrumb mixture.

4 Heat about 1.5cm/½ in of vegetable oil in a large, heavy-based frying pan over low/medium heat. Add the coated turkey burgers and fry them for about 4–5 minutes on each side or until they are brown and crispy on the outside and cooked in the middle.

TROUT WITH CABBAGE & BACON

SERVES 4
20 MINS TO PREPARE • 20 MINS TO COOK

25g/1oz butter, plus
  extra for greasing
1 small onion,
  chopped
3 rashers of smoked
  bacon, cut into
  3mm/⅛in strips

450g/1lb green
  cabbage
6 tsp cider vinegar
8 bay leaves
salt and pepper
4 trout, cleaned, with
  heads removed

1 Melt the butter in a large frying pan. Add the onion and bacon and fry over low heat for 5 minutes or until the onion softens, stirring frequently. Cut the cabbage into thin slices and add this to the pan. Continue frying for a further 10 minutes or until the cabbage softens, stirring often.

2 Stir 2 tsp vinegar into the cabbage mixture, add 4 bay leaves and season with salt and pepper.

3 Meanwhile put 1 tsp of the remaining vinegar and a bay leaf inside the cavity of each fish.

4 Heat the grill to medium. Brush the fish with oil on both sides. Place under the heated grill and cook for 5–8 minutes each side or until the flesh of the fish flakes easily when the point of a knife is inserted at the thickest part.

5 Place the cabbage mixture on a heated serving dish and lay the grilled fish on top. Serve at once.

SERVING IDEAS

Since this dish is served on a bed of vegetables, it doesn't really need an accompaniment, but you could serve it with mashed potato, made with cream and flavoured with a generous pinch of nutmeg.

PAN-FRIED SALMON WITH A HERB SAUCE

SERVES 4
10 MINS TO PREPARE • 15 MINS TO COOK

4 salmon fillets
juice of 1 lemon
salt and pepper
40g/1½oz butter
1 tbls olive oil

FOR THE SAUCE:
2 spring onions,
chopped
50ml/2fl oz
dry white wine

1 tbls capers, finely
chopped
2 tbls finely
chopped fresh
coriander
1 tbls finely
chopped fresh
parsley
200ml/7fl oz
double cream

1 Wash the salmon fillets and pat dry with kitchen towels. Sprinkle with half the lemon juice and add pepper to taste.

2 Melt the butter and oil in a large frying pan over medium-high heat. Add the salmon fillets to the pan, skin sides up, and cook for 3–5 minutes. Turn over and cook for a further 3–5 minutes or until just cooked through – the fish should flake easily when the point of a knife is inserted at the thickest part. Do this in batches, if necessary, then transfer to a serving dish and keep warm.

3 To make the sauce, add the spring onions to the pan, increase the heat to high and pour in the wine. Allow the wine to bubble for 1 minute, then add the capers, coriander, parsley and remaining lemon juice. Stir well, reduce the heat to medium and add the cream. Heat through for 2 minutes, stirrring, but do not allow the sauce to boil. Season with salt and pepper to taste and pour over the salmon. Serve at once.

WHAT TO DRINK

The coriander and capers in the sauce can conflict with your choice of wine. A very crisp white wine, such as Muscadet de Sèvres et Maine, might well be the answer.

PASTA WITH SMOKED SALMON

SERVES 4
15 MINS TO PREPARE • 15 MINS TO COOK

1 tbls olive oil
350g/12oz dried
   tagliarini (or any
   other long pasta)
225g/½lb smoked
   salmon off-cuts
salt and pepper

275ml/½pt
   single cream
2 tbls tomato purée
lemon wedges,
   to serve
   (optional)

1 Bring a large pan of lightly salted water to the boil and add the oil and tagliarini. Bring back to the boil and cook for 8–10 minutes or until tender but still firm to the bite.

2 Meanwhile, using a pair of scissors, trim off any skin or tough bits from the smoked salmon off-cuts and snip into 12mm/½in strips.

3 Pour the cream into a mixing bowl and add the tomato purée. Mix well until evenly coloured.

4 Drain the cooked pasta and return to the pan. Add the tomato cream mixture, the salmon and a generous amount of freshly ground black pepper and place over low heat. Cook, stirring constantly, for 2–3 minutes or until the cream and salmon are heated through. Garnish with lemon wedges, if wished, and serve at once.

SMOKED FISH CHOWDER

SERVES 4
20 MINS TO PREPARE • 25 MINS TO COOK

50g/2oz butter
1 onion, sliced
2 potatoes, diced
450g/1lb smoked
   haddock or cod,
   skinned and cut
   into large chunks

1 bay leaf
275ml/½pt milk
200g/7oz tin
   sweetcorn,
   drained
2 tbls chopped
   parsley

1 Melt the butter in a large saucepan over medium heat. Add the onion and fry for 3 minutes or until slightly softened, stirring often. Add the potatoes and stir well to coat with butter. Reduce the heat to low, cover the pan and cook for 5 minutes, stirring often.

2 Add the fish, bay leaf, milk and 275ml/½pt water. Increase the heat to medium and bring to the boil, then replace the lid and lower the heat. Simmer gently for 15 minutes or until the fish is cooked and the potatoes are tender, stirring now and then.

3 Add the sweetcorn to the chowder and simmer for 2–3 minutes to heat through. Remove the bay leaf and serve hot, sprinkled with the chopped parsley.

WHAT TO DRINK

A New Zealand Sauvignon Blanc, with its herby notes and hint of gooseberry, would go well with this rich soup.

HADDOCK
WITH TOMATO SAUCE

SERVES 4
15 MINS TO PREPARE • 20 MINS TO COOK

1 tbls olive oil	*1 tbls chopped fresh*
10 spring onions,	*mixed herbs or*
thinly sliced	*1 tsp dried*
2 garlic cloves,	*½ tsp ground cumin*
crushed	*salt and pepper*
100g/4oz	*4 haddock fillets,*
mushrooms,	*skinned*
finely chopped	*melted butter, for*
400g/14oz tin	*greasing and*
chopped tomatoes	*brushing*
150ml/5fl oz dry	*basil sprigs, to*
white wine	*garnish (optional)*

1 Heat the oil in a frying pan. Add the spring onions, garlic and mushrooms and cook over medium heat for 5 minutes, stirring frequently. Add the tomatoes, wine, herbs and cumin and season with salt and pepper to taste. Stir well and bring to the boil. Simmer uncovered for 5–10 minutes or until the sauce reduces and thickens slightly.

2 Meanwhile, heat the grill to medium. Grease a grill pan or ovenproof dish with some of the melted butter. Place the haddock fillets in the pan and make two or three diagonal cuts in each piece. Brush the fish with more melted butter and grill for 3–6 minutes each side or until the flesh flakes easily when the point of a knife is inserted at the thickest part. Serve hot with the tomato sauce, garnished with the basil sprigs, if wished.

VARIATIONS

Make the sauce richer by adding cream. At the end of step 1, remove the pan from the heat and stir in 150ml/5fl oz single cream. Reheat gently and adjust the seasoning before serving with the cooked fish.
  Give the sauce an Italian flavour by omitting the mixed herbs and cumin and replacing them with 1 tbls of chopped fresh basil, added at the end of the cooking time.

SMOKED HADDOCK KEDGEREE

SERVES 6
20 MINS TO PREPARE • 30 MINS TO COOK

**700g/1½lb
   smoked haddock
100g/4oz butter
1 large onion, finely
   chopped
225g/½lb
   long-grain rice
2 large pinches of
   curry powder
2 large pinches of
   ground turmeric
3 hard-boiled eggs
juice of ½ lemon
3 tbls chopped
   parsley
salt and pepper
lemon wedges and
   parsley sprigs,
   to garnish**

1 Cut the fish into pieces, if necessary, to fit in a large frying pan or sauté pan. Place the fish in the pan and cover with cold water. Cover and bring to simmering point over medium heat. Then lower the heat and simmer for 10 minutes or until the fish flakes easily when the point of a knife is inserted at the thickest part.

2 Meanwhile, melt 50g/2oz butter in a saucepan and fry the onion over low heat for 2 minutes. Stir in the rice and spices and cook for 1 minute, stirring constantly.

3 Using a fish slice, remove the fish from the frying pan and set aside. Strain the cooking liquid into a measuring jug and add more boiling water, if necessary, to make up to 575ml/1pt. Add to the saucepan and return to the boil, stirring well. Reduce the heat, cover and simmer for 15–20 minutes or until the rice is tender and the liquid has been absorbed.

4 Meanwhile, skin, bone and coarsely flake the fish; chop the eggs coarsely. Remove the rice from the heat and add the remaining butter in small knobs, the fish, eggs, lemon juice and parsley. Return to low heat and gently fork together for 1–2 minutes to heat through. Season to taste (remembering that the fish is salty), transfer to a warm serving dish, garnish and serve at once.

COOK'S TIPS

Kedgeree was first created by Indian cooks during the Victorian era, when Britain ruled India. The dish, which evolved from an Indian mixture of rice and lentils called *kitchri*, combines the British love of smoked fish with Indian culinary traditions. Originally a popular breakfast dish – Victorians ate hearty breakfasts and often had servants to cook them – it is now more appropriate for brunch or supper.

BAKED MACKEREL IN PAPER PARCELS

SERVES 4
15 MINS TO PREPARE • 15 MINS TO COOK

*4 fresh mackerel
fillets (weighing
about 225g/8oz
each)
25mm/1in cube fresh
root ginger, peeled
and finely chopped*

*4 spring onions,
cleaned and
trimmed
1 orange
soy sauce
freshly ground
black pepper*

1 Heat the oven to 180°C/350°F/gas 4. Tear off 4 pieces of non-stick baking paper, each large enough to completely enclose a mackerel fillet. Place each fish fillet in the centre of a piece of paper, skin side down.

2 Sprinkle the chopped ginger over the mackerel fillets. Slice the spring onions and scatter them evenly over each fish.

3 Remove the peel from half the orange, taking care not to include any pith. Cut the peel into shreds and scatter them over the mackerel. Squeeze the juice from the orange and pour about ½ tbls over each fish with a dash of soy sauce and a sprinkling of freshly ground black pepper.

4 Fold the long sides of the paper together, then turn under to form a loose parcel. Twist each end to seal. Place the parcels on a baking sheet and bake for 15 minutes.

5 When the fish has cooked, undo the paper parcels and slide each fish and its juices on to individual serving plates.

WHAT TO DRINK

Complement the spicy flavourings in this dish with a Gewürztraminer.

SWEET-AND-SOUR PRAWNS

SERVES 4
20 MINS TO PREPARE • 10 MINS TO COOK

450g/1lb raw tiger prawns
1 egg
2 tbls cornflour
salt and freshly ground black pepper
oil for deep-frying

FOR THE SAUCE:
1 tbls oil
½ red pepper, de-seeded and cut into small cubes
½ green pepper, de-seeded and cut into small cubes

1 small tin pineapple chunks, drained
2 tbls sugar
3 tbls rice vinegar or cider vinegar
1 tbls light soy sauce
1 tbls rice wine or dry sherry
1 tbls tomato purée
150ml/5fl oz chicken stock
1 tbls cornflour, blended to a paste with water
½ tsp sesame oil (optional)

1 Shell and de-vein the tiger prawns. Beat the egg and cornflour together in a small bowl. Add salt and freshly ground black pepper.

2 Heat the oil in a wok or deep-fat fryer over medium heat. Working in batches, dip the prawns in the egg and cornflour batter and then carefully lower them into the hot fat and deep-fry for about 1–2 minutes. Remove from the fat using a slotted spoon and drain on kitchen towel while you cook the remaining prawns.

3 Heat 1 tbls oil in a clean wok or large, heavy-based pan, then stir-fry the red and green pepper cubes for about 1 minute. Add the pineapple chunks, sugar, vinegar, soy sauce, rice wine or sherry, tomato purée and the chicken stock.

4 Bring to the boil, then cook quickly for 30–40 seconds, stirring constantly. Add the cornflour paste and stir until the sauce thickens, then add the deep-fried prawns and stir for a few seconds more. Sprinkle over the sesame oil, if using. Serve immediately.

VARIATIONS

Instead of prawns, lean pork such as fillet or chops (bones removed), cut into cubes, can be prepared and cooked in exactly the same way. Increase the deep-frying time to about 5 minutes in very hot oil.

STIR-FRIED PRAWNS WITH BROCCOLI

SERVES 4
15 MINS TO PREPARE • 5 MINS TO COOK

225g/8oz broccoli florets
2tbls dry sherry
3 tbls tomato purée
1 tsp sugar
½ tsp Chinese chilli sauce
2 tbls soy sauce
3 tbls oil
225/8oz cooked
  peeled prawns,
  defrosted if frozen
1 tsp finely shredded
  root ginger
1 garlic clove, crushed
1 spring onion,
  thinly sliced

1 Divide the broccoli into small florets. Blanch them in boiling water for 1 minute then drain them well and set them to one side.

2 Combine the sherry, tomato purée, sugar, chilli sauce, soy sauce and 1 tbls of the oil in a small bowl. Mix well.

3 Heat the remaining oil in a wok or heavy frying pan and stir-fry the prawns for about 30 seconds, until they change colour.

4 Add the ginger, garlic and spring onion to the pan and stir-fry for 1 minute. Add the soy sauce mixture and stir-fry for another minute.

5 Add the broccoli florets to the pan and toss over a high heat, then serve immediately.

VARIATIONS

As an alternative, use mangetout instead of the broccoli florets. Use the same weight and top and tail the mangetout before blanching them for 30 seconds.

SIZZLING SEAFOOD KEBABS

SERVES 4
20 MINS TO PREPARE • 5 MINS TO COOK

24 raw tiger prawns
4 shelled scallops
4 large spring onions
lemon wedges and basil sprigs, to garnish

FOR THE MARINADE:
4 tbls olive oil
1 garlic clove, crushed
finely grated zest and juice of ½ lemon
1 tbls finely chopped fresh basil
1 tbls finely chopped fresh coriander
1 tsp clear honey
⅛-¼ tsp sambal oelek, to taste (optional)

1 Remove the shells from the prawns, but leave on the tail pieces. Carefully pick out the black vein that runs along the back of each prawn, pull it away and discard.

2 Remove the scallop corals and cut each scallop in half to give two semi-circles. Cut each spring onion into three pieces.

3 Thread six prawns, two scallop pieces and three pieces of spring onion on to each of four skewers and place on a large plate.

4 Place the marinade ingredients in a small bowl and mix together. Brush some of the marinade mixture over the prepared skewers; reserve the rest. Leave the skewers to marinade until you are ready to cook them.

5 Pre-heat the grill to high and cook the kebabs for 2–3 minutes or until the prawns turn pink and the scallops are firm; don't overcook or they will toughen. As the kebabs cook, brush with more marinade and turn them over. Garnish with lemon wedges and basil sprigs and serve at once.

INGREDIENTS GUIDE

Sambal oelek is a fiery paste made from ground chillies and salt; it is used in Indonesian food. You may find it in some supermarkets or else in speciality shops.

The scallop corals will toughen if used in this recipe, but can be chilled and used in another scallop dish within 12 hours.

TUNA WITH WARM TOMATO SALAD

SERVES 4
15 MINS TO PREPARE • 20 MINS TO COOK

*4 tuna steaks, each
    about 175g/6oz and
    12mm/½in thick
juice of 1 lime
5 tbls olive oil, plus
    extra for greasing
450g/1lb tomatoes
50g/2oz pine nuts*

*1 tbls red pesto
1 tbls red wine
    vinegar
pinch of soft dark
    brown sugar
fresh basil,
    to garnish
lime wedges, to serve*

1 Heat the grill to high and lightly oil the grill rack. Place the tuna steaks on the grill rack. Mix the lime juice and 2 tbls of the oil together. Brush the steaks with the oil and lime mixture and place under the grill. Grill for 8–10 minutes each side or until they flake easily when the point of a knife is inserted at the thickest part.

2 Meanwhile, make the salad: slice the tomatoes and place in a shallow dish. Heat the remaining oil in a frying pan and add the pine nuts. Fry over medium heat for 1 minute or until golden brown, stirring frequently. Remove the nuts from the pan with a slotted spoon and drain on kitchen towels. Set aside.

3 Add the red pesto, vinegar and sugar to the frying pan and stir until well blended. Cook for just a few moments until the sugar has dissolved, stirring all the time.

4 Pour the warm dressing over the tomatoes. Sprinkle with the pine nuts and garnish with basil.

5 Transfer the tuna steaks to warmed serving plates using a fish slice. Serve the tuna with the warm tomato salad and wedges of lime.

TUNA BEAN SALAD

SERVES 4 - 6
20 MINS TO PREPARE • 20 MINS TO COOK

*1 red pepper, halved
    and de-seeded
1 yellow pepper,
    halved and
    de-seeded
225g/8oz green
    beans, trimmed
420g/14½oz tin
    mixed beans
420g/14½oz tin
    flageolet beans
half a large red onion,
    peeled and diced*

*3 tbls bottled
    vinaigrette dressing
    mixed with 1 tbls
    grainy mustard
salt and freshly
    ground black
    pepper
200g/7oz tin of tuna
    in oil, drained
2 tbls thick
    mayonnaise,
    thinned with
    1 tbls milk*

1 Place the pepper halves, cut side down, in a grill pan and cook under a hot grill for about 5–10 minutes. Leave them to cool. When cool, peel off and discard the charred skins and dice the flesh.

2 Cut the green beans into 25mm/1in lengths. Put them in a saucepan of boiling, salted water and boil for 6–8 minutes. Drain, then leave to cool.

3 Drain and rinse the mixed beans and flageolet beans, then mix them together in a bowl with the red onion. Add the green beans and vinaigrette and toss together. Season to taste with salt and freshly ground black pepper.

4 Flake the tuna into a bowl. To serve, arrange the bean mixture on a serving dish, spoon the tuna over the top, then drizzle some of the mayonnaise over the tuna. Sprinkle the diced peppers over the top and serve with the remaining mayonnaise served in a separate bowl.

FUSILLI WITH TUNA & MUSHROOMS

SERVES 6
20 MINS TO PREPARE • 20 MINS TO COOK

salt and pepper
500g/18oz dried
fusilli

FOR THE TOPPING:
2 tbls Parmesan
cheese, grated
3 tbls fresh white
beadcrumbs
cayenne pepper

FOR THE SAUCE:
90g/3½oz butter
50g/2oz plain flour

1.1L/2pt milk
175g/6oz
button mushrooms,
sliced
200g/7oz tin tuna in
brine, drained and
roughly flaked
175g/6oz
Double Gloucester
cheese, grated
2 tbls chopped
fresh parsley
75ml/3fl oz double
cream

1 Bring a large saucepan of salted water to the boil and add the fusilli. Cook for about 10 minutes or until just tender. Drain, then rinse under cold water and drain again.

2 Meanwhile, make the sauce. Melt 50g/2oz butter over low heat, stirring. Add the flour all at once, stirring constantly until it is well blended with the butter. Continue to cook over low heat for 2–3 minutes, stirring constantly. Increase the heat to medium. Gradually add 1.1L/2pt milk, stirring all the time. Continue stirring until the sauce boils and thickens, then lower heat and simmer for 3–4 minutes.

3 While the sauce is simmering, melt the remaining butter in a small saucepan over low heat. Add the mushrooms and cook gently for 2–3 minutes.

4 Using a slotted spoon, transfer the mushrooms to a large, greased ovenproof dish and add the pasta and tuna. Mix well.

5 Remove the white sauce from the heat and stir in the cheese, parsley and cream. Season with salt and pepper to taste. Pour the sauce over the pasta mixture and sprinkle Parmesan, breadcrumbs and cayenne pepper on top.

6 Place under a pre-heated grill for 4–5 minutes or until the topping is golden. Serve at once.

VARIATIONS

You could replace the mushrooms in this recipe with leeks or steamed broccoli florets or a combination of both.

Simply place the vegetables in the top of a steamer and steam until tender but still firm. Add them to the dish with the pasta and the tuna.

TUNA & PEPPER SAVOURY RICE

SERVES 4
20 MINS TO PREPARE • 15 MINS TO COOK

½ green pepper
½ yellow pepper
1 leek
½ tsp olive oil
15g/½oz butter
450g/1lb cooked
    long-grain rice
    (350g/12oz
    uncooked)

1 tsp dried mixed
    herbs
200g/7oz tin tuna,
    drained
2 tsp lemon juice
salt and pepper

1 Using a sharp knife, cut the peppers into thin slices, discarding the seeds and white membranes. Top, tail and slice the leek.

2 Heat the oil and butter in a large frying pan over medium heat. Add the peppers and cook for 3 minutes, stirring. Add the leeks with the mixed herbs and fry for a further 2 minutes.

3 When all the vegetables begin to soften, mix in the cooked rice and the tuna. Cook until the rice and tuna are thoroughly heated through, stirring gently. Just before serving, sprinkle with the lemon juice and season with salt and pepper to taste.

VEGETARIAN OPTIONS

For a vegetarian dish, omit the tuna and add nuts to the cooked rice as an alternative source of protein. Or simply sprinkle the finished dish with grated cheese instead.

QUICK & EASY PIZZAS

SERVES 2
20 MINS TO PREPARE • 15 MINS TO COOK

4 tbls olive oil
2 Spanish onions,
    thinly sliced
2 garlic cloves, crushed
1 round herby
    focaccia bread
    (about 350g/12oz)
2 tbls tomato purée
2 tsp dried mixed
    herbs

350g/12oz tomatoes,
    sliced
50g/2oz
    tin anchovy
    fillets, drained
175g/6oz
    mozzarella cheese,
    sliced
sprigs of basil,
    to garnish

1 Heat the oil in a frying pan over low heat and fry the onions and garlic for 10 minutes or until very soft, stirring often.

2 Cut the focaccia in half horizontally. Spread the cut side of each piece with the tomato purée and sprinkle with the herbs. Cover both pieces of the focaccia with the onion and garlic, then with the slices of tomato.

3 Arrange the anchovy fillets over the tomatoes, then place the cheese slices in the centre of each pizza.

4 Heat the grill to high and put the pizzas under it for 5 minutes or until the cheese bubbles up and browns slightly. Cut into quarters, garnish with sprigs of basil and serve at once.

FRIED HALLOUMI SALAD

SERVES 4 • 15 MINS TO PR RE • 5 MINS TO COOK

1 oak leaf l e
1 head radicchio
1 head frisée
½ head Webb's lettuce
1 yellow pepper,
*   halved, de-seeded*
*   and sliced*
2 tbls sunflower oil
1 tbls walnut oil
100g/4oz walnut
*   pieces*

225g/8oz halloumi
*   cheese*

FOR THE DRESSING:
grated zest and juice
*   of 2 fresh limes*
4 tbls olive oil
2 tbls walnut oil
freshly ground
*   black pepper*

1 Wash the salad leaves in plenty of cold water, then shake off the excess moisture and drain well or pat dry with kitchen towel.

2 Shred the salad leaves and mix them with the strips of pepper in a large serving bowl.

3 To make the dressing, put the lime zest, juice and olive and walnut oils in a screw-top jar. Season to taste with freshly ground black pepper, then put the lid on the jar and shake well to combine the ingredients.

4 Put the sunflower oil and walnut oil in a large, heavy-based frying pan, then add the walnut pieces. Fry for a couple of minutes, then remove the walnuts from the pan using a slotted spoon and leave to drain on kitchen towel.

5 Chop the halloumi cheese into cubes and put them into the frying pan. Fry until all the pieces are lightly browned and crispy.

6 Pour the dressing over the salad leaves in the serving bowl and toss well. Add the walnuts and cheese and serve immediately.

GREEK FETA SALAD

SERVES 4
20 MINS TO PREPARE

4 firm, ripe
tomatoes, cubed
1 green pepper,
de-seeded and
cubed
1 small red onion,
thinly sliced
175g/6oz cucumber,
peeled and cubed
6 radishes,
thinly sliced
2 tbls chopped flat
leaf parsley

1 tbls chopped fresh
oregano
salt and freshly
ground black
pepper
2 - 3 tbls olive oil
150g/5oz feta
cheese, broken into
small chunks
12 pitted black olives

1 Put the tomatoes, green pepper, onion, cucumber and radishes in a large serving bowl. Add the parsley and oregano.

2 Season to taste with salt and freshly ground black pepper, then toss gently. Add enough olive oil just to coat the salad ingredients and toss again.

3 Scatter the chunks of feta cheese and the black olives over the top of the salad and serve immediately.

INGREDIENTS GUIDE

Feta cheese is a milky white, dry, crumbly cheese traditionally made from sheep's milk and preserved in brine. it is quite salty, so you may not need to add salt to the salad at step 2.

BROCCOLI IN A RICH CHEESE SAUCE

SERVES 4 - 6
5 MINS TO PREPARE • 25 MINS TO COOK

**450 - 700g/
 1 - 1½lb broccoli**

FOR THE SAUCE:
75g/3oz butter
75g/3oz flour
850ml/1½pt milk
**2 tsp Dijon
 mustard**
**275g/10oz mild
 Cheddar cheese,
 grated**
**salt and ground
 white pepper**

1 Wash the broccoli, trim away any tough stalks and divide any large heads into smaller ones. Place in boiling salted water and cook for about 8 minutes or until just tender. Drain, place in a serving dish and keep warm.

2 Meanwhile, make the sauce: melt the butter and add the flour, stirring constantly over a low heat for 3 minutes. Increase the heat to medium and gradually add the milk, stirring constantly until the sauce boils and thickens.

3 Simmer over very low heat for 2 minutes, stirring frequently, then remove from the heat and stir in the mustard and 225g/½lb grated cheese. Season to taste, then return the sauce to the heat and simmer gently for 1 minute or until thick and smooth.

4 Pour the cheese sauce over the broccoli and sprinkle with the remaining grated cheese. Place under a medium grill for 5–10 minutes or until the topping is golden and bubbly. Serve immediately.

VARIATIONS

For a crunchier topping, why not mix some toasted almonds or fresh granary breadcrumbs or toasted oatmeal with the grated cheese before putting this dish under the grill?

GRANARY VEGETABLE CRUMBLE

SERVES 4
10 MINS TO PREPARE • 25 MINS TO COOK

175g/6oz
  cauliflower florets
100g/4oz
  broccoli florets
225g/½lb courgettes,
  halved and sliced
1 red pepper,
  coarsely diced
1 large leek,
  halved and sliced
40g/1½oz butter
40g/1½oz flour
425ml/15fl oz milk

1 bunch of
  watercress,
  finely chopped
2 tsp creamed
  horseradish sauce
salt and pepper

FOR THE TOPPING:
50g/2oz butter
50g/2oz
  porridge oats
100g/4oz granary
  breadcrumbs

1 Half-fill the bottom pan of a steamer with water and bring to the boil. Place the cauliflower, broccoli, courgettes, red pepper and leek in the top pan and steam for 5 minutes or until the vegetables are just tender. Turn into an ovenproof dish.

2 Melt the butter in a saucepan and add the flour. Cook over low heat, stirring constantly, for 2 minutes, then increase the heat to medium and gradually add the milk, stirring constantly until the sauce boils and thickens. Simmer over a low heat, stirring frequently, for 3–4 minutes, then remove from the heat and stir in the watercress and the horseradish sauce. Season with salt and pepper to taste. Pour the sauce over the steamed vegetables and mix well.

3 To make the topping, rub the butter into the oats and breadcrumbs, holding your hands high over the bowl and using the tips of your fingers. Sprinkle this evenly over the vegetables and place under a medium grill for 5–10 minutes or until the topping has browned. Serve hot.

COOK'S TIPS

Steaming vegetables rather than boiling them in water has many advantages. Not only do steamed vegetables remain crisper, they retain more of their nutritional value. Also, steamed vegetables won't hold as much moisture as boiled ones. In this recipe, that means that the sauce won't be watered down and the vegetables will keep more of their texture.

CHEESE & TOMATO FONDUE

SERVES 4-6
15 MINS TO PREPARE • 20 MINS TO COOK

450g/1lb new potatoes, unpeeled	**225g/8oz tomatoes, peeled and de-seeded**
1 garlic clove	**2 tsp cornflour**
275g/10oz Swiss Gruyère cheese, grated	**juice of 1 lemon**
275g/10oz Swiss Emmental cheese, grated	**1 tbls tomato purée**
275ml/10fl oz dry white wine	**freshly ground black pepper**
	freshly grated nutmeg

1 Boil the potatoes in a saucepan of salted water for 20 minutes or until soft. Drain and keep warm.

2 Meanwhile cut the garlic clove in half and use it to rub around the inside of a wide, shallow, heatproof pan. Discard the garlic clove. Add the grated cheeses, wine and tomatoes to the pan.

3 Mix the cornflour with the lemon juice and add to the cheese mixture. Place the pan over low heat and gently bring the contents to the boil, stirring constantly.

4 Stir in the tomato purée and simmer for 3–4 minutes, then remove the pan from the heat and season to taste with black pepper and nutmeg. Transfer the pan to a spirit burner at the table.

5 Put the warm potatoes in a napkin-lined basket and serve with the fondue. Spear each potato with a long fork or specialist fondue fork, then dip the potato into the hot cheese mixture before eating.

TOOLS OF THE TRADE

The word fondue is derived from the Latin *fundere*, to pour, and the French *fondre*, to melt, so you need a dish in which the cheese can be melted and then retained at pouring consistency. Traditionally, the Swiss use a *caquelon*, an earthenware pot which cooks the cheese very slowly without overheating it. Overheating tends to make the cheese stringy. If you don't have a fondue set or *caquelon*, use a wide, shallow pan made of earthenware, enamelled cast iron or any other heatproof material, plus a spirit burner for the table.

BEAN & VEGETABLE PIE

SERVES 4
25 MINS TO PREPARE • 25 MINS TO COOK

1 tbls vegetable oil
1 onion, finely chopped
1 clove garlic, crushed
225g/½lb button mushrooms, halved
350g/12oz courgettes, halved lengthways and cut into 3mm/⅛in slices
3 tbls flour
150ml/5fl oz vegetable stock,
150ml/5fl oz milk

440g/1lb tin red kidney beans, drained and rinsed
440g/1lb tin cannellini beans, drained and rinsed
salt and pepper
2 tbls chopped fresh parsley
450g/1lb potatoes, cut into 6mm/¼in slices
175g/6oz red Leicester cheese, grated

1 Heat the oil in a large saucepan over medium heat and add the onion and garlic. Fry for 5 minutes or until soft. Add the mushrooms and cook for 2 minutes, stirring occasionally. Add the courgettes, sprinkle on the flour and mix well. Cook for 2–3 minutes, stirring constantly.

2 Mix the stock and milk in a jug, then gradually add to the pan, stirring. Continue to cook until the sauce boils and thickens, then simmer over low heat for 3–4 minutes, stirring frequently. Mix in the two kinds of beans and the parsley and season to taste. Spoon the mixture into a casserole or flameproof serving dish and keep warm.

3 Meanwhile, put the potatoes into a pan of salted water and bring to the boil. Cook for 5 minutes or until tender. Drain and arrange on top of the bean mixture. Sprinkle with the cheese and place under a moderate grill until the cheese browns. Serve hot.

CANNELLINI BEANS & TOMATOES

SERVES 4
5 MINS TO PREPARE • 15 MINS TO COOK

2 x 400g/14oz tins cannellini beans, drained and rinsed
5 sage leaves
4 tbls olive oil
salt and freshly ground black pepper

2 garlic cloves, thinly sliced
1 x 400g/14oz tin chopped Italian plum tomatoes
sage leaves, to garnish

1 Heat the oil in a large, heavy-based saucepan. Add the garlic and sage leaves, then cook for 1 minute to flavour the oil.

2 Add the tomatoes, cover the pan and cook for 10 minutes over medium heat. Then add the beans. Season generously with salt and freshly ground black pepper and cook until the beans are heated through. Garnish with sage leaves before serving.

SERVING IDEAS

This dish is very quick and simple to make. For a filling main course, serve it with crusty bread and a green salad or pasta bows tossed in olive oil. If beans are eaten with bread or pasta, they will provide as much protein as is found in meat or fish.

SPICY BEAN BURRITOS

SERVES 4
20 MINS TO PREPARE • 20 MINS TO COOK

8 soft flour tortillas

FOR THE FILLING:
2 tbls vegetable oil
1 large onion, chopped
2 garlic cloves, crushed
2 x 430g/15½oz tins red kidney beans in chilli sauce

100g/4oz Cheddar cheese, coarsely grated
150ml/5fl oz soured cream
½ iceberg lettuce, shredded
4 tomatoes, chopped
4 spring onions, chopped

1 Heat the oil in a saucepan over medium heat and fry the onion and garlic for 10 minutes or until golden, stirring often. Add the beans and heat through, stirring occasionally. Mash with a potato masher or fork and keep warm.

2 Bring a saucepan of water to the boil, lower the heat to a simmer and place a heatproof plate on top. Heat a 25cm/10in non-stick frying pan over medium heat. Put the tortillas, one at a time, into the pan and heat for 30 seconds each side. Transfer the tortillas to the plate over the pan to keep warm and cover with greaseproof paper. Continue in this way until all the tortillas are heated and stacked on the plate, with a sheet of grease-proof paper between each.

3 To assemble the burritos, lay a tortilla on your work surface and place 3 tbls bean mixture in the centre. Top with 2 tbls cheese, 1 tbls soured cream and some lettuce, tomato and spring onion. Fold opposite sides of the tortilla to meet in the centre, then fold one end under. Transfer to a warm serving dish. Continue until all the tortillas are filled. Serve warm.

INGREDIENTS GUIDE

Tortillas are round, thin cakes of unleavened corn-meal or wheat flour. They can be bought ready-made from any large supermarket.

CHANNA DHAL WITH PEPPERS

SERVES 4 - 6
20 MINS TO PREPARE • 25 MINS TO COOK

4 tbls vegetable oil
1 tsp mustard seeds
½ tsp cumin seeds
¼ tsp asafoetida (optional)
1 onion, finely chopped
3 garlic cloves, crushed
2 tsp ground cumin seeds from 5 cardamom pods, crushed
½ tsp ground turmeric

1½ tsp salt
1 tsp sugar
2 tomatoes, skinned and chopped
2 x 400g/14oz tins channa dhal or chick peas
1 red pepper, de-seeded and diced
1 green pepper, de-seeded and diced
fresh coriander leaves, to garnish

1 Heat the oil in a large, heavy-based saucepan. Add the mustard and cumin seeds and the asafoetida, if using, and stir-fry gently until the seeds begin to pop. Add the onion and fry gently for a further 5–7 minutes until it turns golden.

2 Add the garlic, ground cumin, cardamom and turmeric. Stir for 1 minute, then add the salt, sugar and tomatoes. Cook for a further 2 minutes.

3 Drain the tinned dhal or chick peas and add them to the pan. Bring to the boil, then simmer gently over low heat for about 10 minutes. Add extra water to the pan if the mixture is too thick.

4 Add the peppers and simmer for 5 minutes. Turn into a serving dish and garnish with coriander before serving.

JAMAICAN RICE & PEAS

SERVES 6
15 MINS TO PREPARE • 25 MINS TO COOK

400g/14oz tin gunga peas or red kidney beans	**½ fresh chilli, seeded and finely sliced**
200g/7oz compressed creamed coconut	**1 garlic clove, crushed**
1.2L/2¼pt boiling water	**1 spring onion, sliced salt and pepper**
few sprigs of thyme	**350g/12oz long-grain rice, rinsed**

1 Drain the beans in a colander and discard the water. Rinse under cold running water.

2 Cut the block of creamed coconut into chunks and place in a large saucepan over medium heat. Pour on the boiling water and stir well until dissolved.

3 Add the thyme, chilli, garlic and spring onion and season with salt and pepper to taste. Simmer for 2–3 minutes, then stir in the rice.

4 Return to the boil, cover and simmer very gently for 15–20 minutes or until the rice is tender. Add the beans and leave just enough time for them to heat through. Serve at once.

NUTRITION NOTES

The combination of pulse and grain makes this dish a good source of first class protein; it is also full of fibre and B vitamins.

EGG-FRIED RICE

SERVES 4
10 MINS TO PREPARE • 5 MINS TO COOK

2 eggs	**450g/1lb cooked long-grain rice**
1 tsp salt	**100g/4oz peas, fresh or frozen**
2 spring onions, finely chopped	
2 - 3 tbls vegetable oil	

1 Put the eggs in a bowl, add a pinch of the salt and half the spring onions and lightly beat together.

2 Heat the oil in a pre-heated wok or large, heavy-based frying pan. Add the egg mixture and stir until the eggs are lightly scrambled.

3 Add the rice and stir to make sure that each grain of rice is separated. Add the peas with the remaining salt and all but ½ tbls of the remaining spring onions, then blend together well and stir-fry for 2–3 minutes.

4 Serve the egg-fried rice hot or cold, garnished with the reserved spring onions.

COOK'S TIPS

The rice used for this recipe should not be too soft. Ideally, it should have been slightly under-cooked and left to cool before frying.

At step 2 the eggs should be scrambled until they are slightly set but still moist. Don't cook for too long or they will turn rubbery.

SZECHWAN VEGETABLE NOODLES

SERVES 4
15 MINS TO PREPARE • 10 MINS TO COOK

*200g/7oz rice
vermicelli
(or 250g/9oz egg
noodles)*
*100g/4oz tinned
Szechwan
preserved
vegetable*
4 tbls oil
2 tbls light soy sauce
*100g/4oz tinned
sliced bamboo
shoots, drained
and shredded*
*2 - 3 spring onions,
shredded*
*1 - 2 small fresh red
chillies, de-seeded
and finely shredded*
1 tsp sesame oil

1 Soak the rice noodles in boiling water for 6–8 minutes. Rinse in cold water and drain thoroughly.

2 Wash the Szechwan preserved vegetable, then finely shred.

3 Heat the oil in a pre-heated wok or large, heavy-based frying pan, then add the noodles and stir-fry them with the soy sauce for 1–1½ minutes.

4 Add the preserved vegetable, bamboo shoots and spring onions and stir until well mixed. Sprinkle with the red chillies and drizzle the sesame oil over the top. Serve hot or cold.

INGREDIENTS GUIDE

Obtainable from specialist Chinese or Oriental supermarkets and delicatessens, Szechwan preserved vegetable is a pickled mustard root and it tastes very hot and salty. Washing it before use takes the edge off the heat without losing flavour. It is sold in tins, and once opened the preserved vegetable will keep for many months if stored in a tightly sealed jar in the fridge. Sometimes preserved vegetable can be obtained ready-shredded.

MALAYSIAN EGG NOODLES

SERVES 4
20 MINS TO PREPARE • 20 MINS TO COOK

1 tbls vegetable oil
1 onion, peeled and
    sliced
2 garlic cloves,
    crushed
2.5cm/1in piece fresh
    root ginger,
    finely chopped
850ml/1½pt
    vegetable stock
salt and freshly
ground black pepper
100g/4oz cabbage
    leaves, shredded
1 fresh or dried red
    chilli, finely
    chopped (optional)
225g/8oz
    egg noodles
75g/3oz
    bean sprouts
2 spring onions,
    chopped
soy sauce

1 Heat the oil in a large, heavy-based saucepan. Add the sliced onion and crushed garlic and stir-fry until the onion is soft.

2 Add the chopped ginger and vegetable stock and season to taste with salt and freshly ground black pepper.

3 Bring to the boil, then reduce the heat, cover and simmer gently for 10 minutes. Add the cabbage leaves and chilli (if using), then increase the heat and bring the mixture to a gentle rolling boil.

4 Add the egg noodles, bean sprouts and spring onions, then stir in soy sauce to taste.

5 Adjust the seasoning, then leave the soup to simmer, covered, for 5–7 minutes or until the noodles are cooked. Transfer the contents of the pan to a serving dish and garnish (see Serving Ideas).

SERVING IDEAS

Traditional garnishes include sliced hard-boiled eggs, thin strips of omelette, tomato wedges, finely chopped celery tops or fried onion rings.

SWEET-AND-SOUR VEGETABLES

SERVES 4
20 MINS TO PREPARE • 10 MINS TO COOK

*1 tbls cornflour
1 tbls light
  soy sauce
25ml/1fl oz white
  wine vinegar
150ml/5fl oz
  pineapple juice
1 tbls tomato purée
25g/1oz soft light
  brown sugar
2 tbls vegetable oil
1 garlic clove, peeled
  and crushed
2.5cm/1in cube of
  fresh root ginger,
  finely chopped
100g/4oz
  broccoli florets*

*225g/8oz carrots,
  peeled and cut
  into strips
100g/4oz baby
  sweetcorn, cut in
  half lengthways
12 spring onions,
  halved and cut into
  5cm/2in strips
100g/4oz mangetout,
  topped and tailed
  and cut in half
  lengthways
200g/7oz bean shoots
2 tbls toasted
  sesame seeds
egg noodles or rice,
  to serve*

1 Blend the cornflour and soy sauce together with the white wine vinegar. Add the pineapple juice, tomato purée, soft light brown sugar and 75ml/3fl oz water. Stir well to mix, then set aside.

2 Heat the vegetable oil in a large, heavy-based frying pan or wok, then stir in the garlic and ginger. Fry over high heat for 30 seconds, then add the broccoli, carrots and sweetcorn. Stir-fry for 3 minutes.

3 Stir in the spring onions, mangetout and bean shoots, then add the pineapple juice mixture. Bring to the boil and stir until thickened, then simmer for 2 minutes.

4 Scatter the toasted sesame seeds over the top and serve immediately with egg noodles or rice.

CRISP GREEN STIR-FRY

SERVES 4
15 MINS TO PREPARE • 10 MINS TO COOK

*175g/6oz
  broccoli
350g/12oz
  courgettes
100g/4oz
  mangetout
4 spring onions
3 tbls peanut oil*

*25mm/1in cube
  fresh root ginger,
  peeled and
  grated
2 garlic cloves,
  finely chopped
2 tbls oyster sauce
2 tbls chicken stock*

1 Split the broccoli spears in half lengthways and cut into walnut-size pieces. Quarter the courgettes lengthways and cut into chunks. Top and tail the mangetout. Cut the spring onions into pieces 12mm/½in long.

2 In a preheated wok, heat the oil over high heat and stir-fry the ginger for 30 seconds. Add the garlic and the broccoli and stir-fry for 1 minute.

3 Add the courgettes and stir-fry for a further 1½ minutes. Add the spring onions and mangetout and cook for 1 minute, stirring constantly.

4 Stir in the oyster sauce and chicken stock and cook for 2 minutes, stirring constantly. Serve at once.

SERVING IDEAS

Fresh vegetables play an important part in any healthy diet, being full of a wide variety of vitamins and minerals as well as a good source of fibre. Green vegetables are high in vitamin C and contain useful amounts of calcium and iron.

CATALAN OMELETTE

SERVES 4
15 MINS TO PREPARE • 10 MINS TO COOK

6 tomatoes, skinned	*salt and pepper*
2 green peppers	*8 large eggs*
1 red pepper	*2 large egg*
3 tbls olive oil	*whites*
3 shallots, finely	*6 black olives,*
chopped	*stoned*
3 garlic cloves,	*1 tbls finely*
finely chopped	*chopped parsley*

1 Chop the tomatoes coarsely, discarding seeds and juice. Cut the peppers in half, de-seed them then cut into strips.

2 Heat 2 tbls oil in a frying pan and add the peppers, shallots and garlic. Fry over low heat until the shallots are soft and transparent and the peppers still crisp. Add the tomatoes, season with salt and pepper to taste and cook for a few more minutes stirring from time to time.

3 Break the eggs into a mixing bowl and season with salt and pepper. Beat lightly with a fork.

4 Put the egg whites in a large, clean, dry bowl with a pinch of salt and whisk to soft peaks. Gently fold them into the beaten eggs.

5 Heat the remaining 1 tbls oil in a 23cm/9in omelette pan and pour in the eggs. Stir the mixture gently with the back of a fork, letting the liquid egg run to the sides so that the omelette cooks evenly. Then leave undisturbed to cook for a few seconds until the omelette is just set but still moist. Remove from the heat.

6 Pour the vegetable mixture onto a warmed serving dish. Fold the omelette in half and slide it on top. Garnish the omelette with olives and chopped parsley. Serve hot.

EGGS FLORENTINE

SERVES 4
10 MINS TO PREPARE • 25 MINS TO COOK

700g/1½lb spinach
75g/3oz butter
salt and pepper
½ tsp grated nutmeg
3 tbls flour
275ml/½pt milk
100g/4oz mature
   Cheddar cheese,
   grated
4 eggs
¼ tsp vinegar
25g/1oz fresh brown
   breadcrumbs

1 Wash the spinach, discarding any tough stalks and bruised leaves. Put 25g/1oz of the butter into a large saucepan, add the spinach and push down well. Cover and cook over medium heat for 6–8 minutes, turning the spinach from time to time so that it cooks evenly. When the spinach is cooked, remove from the pan and chop.

2 Cover the bottom of a shallow gratin dish with the chopped spinach and place it in the oven to keep warm while you make the sauce.

3 Melt the remaining butter in a small pan. Add the flour, stirring constantly over a low heat for 3 minutes. Increase the heat to medium and gradually add the milk, stirring constantly until the sauce boils and thickens. Turn down the heat and add the grated cheese. Cook until the cheese has melted, stirring constantly. Turn off the heat and leave to stand while you poach the eggs, stirring the sauce occasionally to prevent a skin forming.

4 To poach the eggs, half fill a small saucepan with water, add a little salt and the vinegar. Bring to simmering point over a medium heat, then reduce to low heat. Crack one egg into a bowl and use a large metal spoon to slide it into the water. Repeat for the other eggs. Poach in simmering water for 3–4 minutes. Heat the grill to medium.

5 Remove the spinach from the oven. Use a slotted spoon to remove the eggs from the pan and place them on top of the spinach. Pour the cheese sauce over them. Sprinkle the breadcrumbs on top, then place under the grill until golden. Serve at once.

FUSILLI & LEEK BAKE

SERVES 4 - 6
20 MINS TO PREPARE • 25 MINS TO COOK

50g/2oz butter
450g/1lb leeks,
   trimmed and sliced
   into 12mm/½in
   lengths
50g/2oz flour
425ml/15fl oz milk
425ml/15fl oz
   vegetable stock
100g/4oz strong
   Cheddar cheese,
   grated

salt and freshly
   ground black
   pepper
300g/11oz yellow
   courgettes, grated
300g/11oz fusilli
100g/4oz fresh
   breadcrumbs
100g/4oz grated
   Parmesan cheese

1 Melt the butter in a large heavy-based saucepan over low heat. Add the leeks, then cover and cook for 10 minutes or until the leeks are tender, stirring occasionally to prevent them from sticking to the bottom of the pan.

2 Sprinkle in the flour and stir until it has absorbed all the buttery juices. Gradually add the milk and vegetable stock, stirring constantly.

3 Add the grated Cheddar cheese and stir into the leek sauce. Season to taste with salt and freshly ground black pepper, then remove the pan from the heat and stir in the grated courgettes.

4 Meanwhile cook the fusilli in a large pan of salted boiling water until it is cooked but not soft. Drain and tip it into a large ovenproof dish, then pour the cheesy leek sauce over the top and mix together.

5 Combine the breadcrumbs and Parmesan cheese, then spoon the mixture over the pasta in one thick layer. Place the dish under a pre-heated grill until the topping is browned and the pasta has heated through thoroughly.

WHAT TO DRINK

This is a very comforting pasta dish, and needs an unassuming, light, crisp white wine to complement it. An Italian Orvieto, a Muscadet or a Californian white wine would all go well.

PASTA WITH GARLIC, OIL & HOT CHILLI

SERVES 4
5 MINS TO PREPARE • 15 MINS TO COOK

400g/14oz linguine, spaghetti or vermicelli
125ml/4fl oz olive oil
3 garlic cloves, very finely chopped

3 tbls chopped parsley
1 dry chilli, crushed
salt
Parmesan cheese, finely grated (optional)

1 Bring 4L/1.7pt of water to the boil. Add 1 tsp salt. As soon as the water boils rapidly, add all the pasta at once. Do not break the long pasta, but ease it gently as it becomes soft. Stir thoroughtly to prevent the pasta from sticking together. Cover the pan, bring the water back to the boil, then remove the lid as soon as the water boils. Stir again, then adjust the heat so that the water boils fast without boiling over.

2 Meanwhile, prepare the sauce. Heat the oil in a large frying pan or a large shallow saucepan over medium heat, add the garlic, parsley and chilli and cook for 2 minutes, stirring constantly. Be careful not to burn the garlic.

3 Test the pasta and drain it as soon as it is *al dente* – cooked but firm to the bite. Strain it in a colander and give 2 or 3 brisk shakes, but be careful not to overdrain or it will become too dry.

4 Add the pasta to the frying pan and cook it over medium-low heat for 2 minutes, stirring all the time. Serve at once with Parmesan cheese to sprinkle over the top if you want.

PASTA WITH TOMATOES & PINE NUTS

SERVES 4
15 MINS TO PREPARE • 10 MINS TO COOK

700g/1½lb ripe plum tomatoes
1 garlic clove
2 tsp caster sugar
2 tbls chopped fresh basil
50g/2oz pine nuts
2 tbls tomato purée

5 tbls olive oil
salt and pepper
350g/12oz dried fettucine
freshly grated Parmesan cheese, to serve (optional)

1 Put the tomatoes in a bowl and cover with boiling water. Leave for 2 minutes. Remove, and if the skins have not split, pierce with a fork or skewer. Peel away the skins before the tomatoes get too cold, cut in half and scoop out the seeds. Roughly chop 225g/½lb tomatoes and set aside.

2 Place the remaining tomatoes in a food processor or blender together with the garlic, sugar, 1 tbls basil, pine nuts and tomato purée. Process until the sauce is smooth.

3 Continue blending at slow speed while you pour in 4 tbls olive oil in a thin, steady stream. When thickened, pour into a non-metallic bowl and add the chopped tomatoes.

4 Bring a large pan of salted water to the boil and add the remaining oil, then the pasta. Return to the boil and cook for 8 minutes or until firm to the bite. Turn off the heat. Drain the pasta, return to the pan and immediately stir in the tomato sauce.

5 To serve, spoon the pasta into warmed dishes and scatter with the remaining basil. Serve at once, with grated Parmesan cheese if liked.

WHAT TO DRINK

Drink a light, fruity Italian wine with this simple pasta dish – a Bardolino would be ideal.

TORTELLINI IN CORIANDER CREAM

SERVES 4
10 MINS TO PREPARE • 15 MINS TO COOK

salt and pepper
350g/12oz dried
*   tortellini*
15g/½oz butter
1 tbls olive oil
½ onion, finely
*   chopped*
1 garlic clove,
*   crushed*
2 tsp cornflour
275ml/½pt double
*   cream*
100g/4oz Parmesan
*   cheese, grated*
2 tbls chopped fresh
*   coriander leaves*
2 tbls chopped
*   fresh parsley*
fresh coriander
*   sprigs, to garnish*
*   (optional)*

1 Bring a large saucepan of salted water to the boil and and add the tortellini. Cooking times may vary so follow the instructions on the packet.

2 Meanwhile, heat the butter and oil in a saucepan and fry the onion and garlic for 5 minutes or until the onion is soft and translucent, stirring frequently.

3 Mix the cornflour to a smooth paste with 1 tbls water. Lower the heat, stir in the cream, cheese and cornflour paste and cook for 4–5 minutes or until slightly thickened, stirring constantly. Add most of the coriander and parsley and season with salt and pepper to taste.

4 As soon as it is cooked, drain the tortellini and transfer to heated serving dishes. Pour over the sauce and sprinkle with the remaining chopped herbs. Garnish with sprigs of coriander, if wished, and serve at once.

INGREDIENTS GUIDE

Tortellini are little pockets of pasta, available fresh or dried and with a variety of fillings. The dried ones make a perfect storecupboard standby. Choose a vegetable or cheese filling to complement this sauce and follow the cooking instructions printed on the packet for perfect results.

PASTA, GREEN BEAN & COURGETTE SALAD

SERVES 4
15 MINS TO PREPARE • 15 MINS TO COOK

salt
275g/10oz
   pasta shells
1 tbls olive oil
175g/6oz green
   beans
1 large courgette,
   cut into thin
   2cm/¾in-long strips
½ red onion, peeled
   and finely chopped
15g/½oz pine nuts,
   toasted

FOR THE DRESSING:
150ml/5fl oz
   mayonnaise
8 tbls single cream
2 tsp lemon juice
finely grated zest
   of 1 lemon
4 tbls finely chopped
   flat-leaved parsley
2 tbls finely chopped
   fresh mixed herbs
   such as thyme,
   basil and rosemary
freshly ground
   black pepper

1 Boil a large pan of salted water, add the pasta shells and cook until soft, or according to the instructions on the packet. Drain, then transfer to a large bowl and stir in the olive oil to prevent the pasta sticking together. Leave to cool.

2 Plunge the green beans in boiling salted water for 1 minute, then drain and chop. Add to the pasta with the courgette strips and onion.

3 Combine the dressing ingredients in a bowl. Spoon over the salad and toss well. Sprinkle with the pine nuts just before serving.

COOK'S TIPS

To toast the pine nuts, spread them out in a small roasting tin and put in an oven heated to 180°C/350°F/gas 4 for 3–5 minutes or until golden.

LINGUINI WITH TOMATO SAUCE

SERVES 4-6
10 MINS TO PREPARE • 25 MINS TO COOK

4 tbls olive oil
1 onion, finely
   chopped
2 garlic cloves,
   crushed
400g/14oz tin
   chopped tomatoes
salt and pepper
½-1 tsp sugar

1-2 tsp dried
   oregano, basil or
   marjoram
450g/1lb linguini
basic sprigs to
   garnish
freshly grated
   Parmesan,
   to serve

1 Heat the oil in a saucepan, add the onion and garlic and cook over low heat for 5 minutes or until the onion is soft but not brown, stirring occasionally.

2 Add the tomatoes and their juice, salt and pepper to taste, the sugar and the herbs. Stir well, cover and simmer gently for 10 minutes, stirring occasionally.

3 Remove the cover and continue simmering for a further 10 minutes to allow the sauce to reduce slightly.

4 Meanwhile, cook the linguini until *al dente*. Drain thoroughly and transfer to a heated serving dish.

5 Pour the tomato sauce over the pasta, garnish with basil and serve immediately, with Parmesan cheese.

DESSERTS

These delicious recipes show that home-made
desserts need not take long to prepare.
Most contain fresh fruit so are not only quick
but healthy as well.

FRESH FRUIT & ORANGE CREAM

SERVES 4
15 MINS TO PREPARE • 10 MINS TO COOK

2 oranges
4 tbls caster sugar
100ml/4fl oz
   Cointreau (optional)
6 nectarines, peeled
   and stoned

225g/8oz
   fresh blueberries
275ml/½pt
   double cream

1 Grate the zest from one orange and peel fine strips of zest off the other using a zester.

2 Squeeze the juice of the oranges into a small saucepan and add the sugar. Heat gently over medium heat until the sugar has dissolved, stirring occasionally. Add the Cointreau.

3 Place the nectarines and blueberries in a bowl. Pour the orange syrup over the fruit.

4 Meanwhile whip the cream, adding the grated zest. Put the cream in a serving bowl, and use the strips of orange zest to decorate the top.

5 Spoon the fruit into individual serving dishes and top with the cream, or serve in a large dish and serve the cream separately.

NUTRITION NOTES

Yellow fruits such as nectarines are rich in carotene which is converted to vitamin A in the body. Oranges and blueberries are rich in vitamin C. If you want to reduce the calorie content of this dessert, leave out the double cream.

SCOTTISH RASPBERRY CRANACHAN

SERVES 6
15 MINS TO PREPARE • 10 MINS TO COOK

75g/3oz medium
   oatmeal
425ml/15fl oz
   double cream
150ml/5fl oz
   single cream

2 tbls whisky
3 - 4 tbls
   clear honey
350g/12oz
   raspberries

1 Spread the oatmeal on a baking tray. Place it under a heated grill for 6–8 minutes or until the oatmeal is golden brown, shaking the tray every 30 seconds to prevent burning. Transfer to a bowl and leave to cool.

2 Mix the double and single creams together, stir in the whisky and 2 tbls of the honey. Stir in the oatmeal, mixing well.

3 Reserve some of the best fresh raspberries, then fold the rest into the cream mixture.

4 Spoon the mixture into glass serving dishes, decorate with the reserved fresh raspberries and drizzle with the remaining honey before serving.

TEQUILA &
PINEAPPLE DELIGHT

SERVES 4
15 MINS TO PREPARE • 20 MINS TO COOK

50g/2oz blanched almonds
1 small pineapple
4 tbls ground almonds
3 egg yolks
4 tbls sugar

3 tbls tequila
4 trifle sponges
3 tbls apricot jam
225ml/8fl oz crème fraîche

1 Heat the grill to high. Place a piece of foil over the wire rack in the grill pan and sprinkle the almonds on evenly. Toast for 1 minute or until lightly browned, stirring and watching closely to make sure they do not burn. Leave to cool.

2 Peel the pineapple and cut into quarters. Cut away the central core from each piece and discard. Finely chop the flesh and put into a saucepan. Add the ground almonds, egg yolks, sugar and 2 tbls tequila and place the pan over medium heat. Cook until the mixture thickens, stirring constantly. Transfer to a bowl and set aside.

3 Cut the trifle sponges in half. Using 2 tbls apricot jam, spread jam over the cut side of each sponge half.

4 Cover the base of a serving dish with half the jam-covered sponges, overlapping them if necessary, and sprinkle ½ tbls tequila over them. Spoon half the pineapple mixture over the sponges. Add another layer of sponge halves, jam sides up, and sprinkle with the remaining tequila. Cover with the remaining pineapple mixture. Spread the crème fraîche over the top of the dessert.

5 Heat 1 tbls apricot jam with 1 tbls water in a small saucepan over low heat to make a thin syrup, stirring constantly. Drizzle this over the dessert, using a spoon to swirl it lightly into the cream. Scatter the almonds on top.

INGREDIENTS GUIDE

Tequila is a clear spirit made in Mexico from a cactus-like plant called the agave. Juice is extracted, left to ferment, then distilled to make a highly alcoholic drink. Tequila can be clear or a golden colour, depending on how it is aged. In Mexico, it is traditional to drink the tequila in one gulp, accompanied by a slice of lime and a pinch of salt. You can buy tequila in miniature bottles and there is enough in one for this dessert. If you can't get tequila, then substitute Cointreau or white rum.

Crème fraîche is a slightly acidic cream which originated in France. If you can't find any, use soured cream instead.

PLEASE NOTE
This dessert contains lightly cooked egg yolks, so should be avoided by young children, pregnant women, nursing mothers, the elderly and those suffering from immune deficiency diseases.

QUICK FRUIT BRÛLÉE

SERVES 4
10 MINS TO PREPARE • 25 MINS TO COOK

500g/18oz fresh apricots
sugar syrup made using 50g/2oz caster sugar dissolved in 275ml/½pt warm water
25mm/1in cinnamon stick
2 bay leaves
250g/9oz mascarpone cheese
275ml/½pt single cream
1 tbls caster sugar
75g/3oz demerara sugar
1 tsp cinnamon
bay leaf, to decorate

VARIATIONS

You can also make this dish using a 400g/14oz tin of apricot halves and 75ml/3fl oz apricot brandy. Heat the apricots and their juice in a saucepan with the brandy. Remove the apricots from the pan and transfer to a serving dish, then proceed as for fresh apricots from step 2.

1 Halve and stone the apricots. Put them in a saucepan with the sugar syrup, cinnamon stick and 2 bay leaves. Cover, put the pan over medium heat and simmer for 10 minutes. Remove the apricots from the pan and transfer them to a serving dish, arranging them so that they are in a single layer.

2 Return the pan to the heat and boil until the liquid has reduced to a syrup. Pour the syrup over the apricots.

3 Heat the grill to medium. Combine the mascarpone cheese, cream and caster sugar, then spoon the mixture over the apricots.

4 Mix the demerara sugar with the cinnamon and sprinkle evenly over the mascarpone and cream mixture, then put the dish under the grill, and cook for 5–10 minutes or until the sugar has caramelized. Serve immediately.

BANANAS FRIED
WITH RAISINS

SERVES 4
5 MINS TO PREPARE • 10 MINS TO COOK

40g/1½oz butter
3 tbls demerara
sugar
50g/2oz raisins

1 tbls lemon juice
4 firm, slightly under-
ripe bananas

1 Melt the butter in a large frying pan over low heat, add the sugar and stir until dissolved. Add the raisins and lemon juice to the pan and cook for 3 minutes, stirring constantly.

2 Meanwhile, peel the bananas and cut them in half; cut these pieces in half lengthways.

3 Add to the pan and cook for 5 minutes, turning occasionally to coat with the sauce. Serve immediately, accompanied by cream or ice cream.

WHAT TO DRINK

If you'd like something to drink with this warming dessert, then try a glass of Armagnac or a tot of rum.

RAISIN SEMOLINA

SERVES 4-6
10 MINS TO PREPARE • 20 MINS TO COOK

600ml/1 pint milk
40g/1½oz semolina
40g/1½oz seedless raisins
1 egg, beaten
50g/2oz Demerara sugar

½ teaspoon ground cinnamon
15g/½ oz margarine or butter shaved into flakes
margarine or butter, for greasing

1 Brush the inside of 6 ramekin dishes with margarine.

2 Pour the milk into a heavy-based saucepan and heat gently until just below boiling point. Sprinkle in the semolina and stir until the mixture comes to the boil. Add the raisins and reduce the heat and cook gently for 15 minutes, stirring frequently.

3 Remove the pan from the heat. Leave the semolina mixture to cool slightly, then beat in the egg, a little at a time. Return the pan to low heat and cook, stirring, for 1 minute. Heat the grill to high.

4 Turn the semolina mixture into the prepared dishes and level the surface. Mix the sugar with the cinnamon and sprinkle over the puddings, then dot with the margarine or butter.

5 Place the dishes under the grill for 2–3 minutes, until the sugar is melted and bubbling. Serve hot or cold with whipped cream, if desired.

GREEN FRUIT SALAD

SERVES 4
15 MINS TO PREPARE

2 kiwifruit
100g/4oz seedless green grapes, well rinsed and wiped dry
150g/5oz green-fleshed melon such as honeydew

12 tinned lychees, drained
1 large Granny Smith apple, well rinsed and wiped dry
2 limes
1 - 2 tsp caster sugar
mint leaves to garnish

1 Peel the kiwifruit. Chop them into chunks and put them into a glass serving bowl. Halve the grapes and add them to the bowl with the drained lychees.

2 Cut the melon in half and remove the seeds. Use a melon baller to scoop the flesh into balls, or cut the flesh into bite-sized chunks. Quarter and core the apple. Thinly slice the quarters and add to the bowl.

3 Pare some of the zest from the limes and reserve for the garnish. Finely grate the remaining lime zest over the fruit in the bowl and sprinkle with the sugar.

4 Squeeze the juice from 1½ of the limes into the bowl and mix until the fruit is lightly coated with the juice. Add more sugar or lime juice to taste.

5 Cover the bowl and chill until ready to serve. Spoon into individual dishes. Garnish with fine curls of lime zest and mint leaves.

VARIATIONS

Once very expensive, lychees are now sold in most large supermarkets. If you are going to use fresh lychees you will need to peel them by splitting open the pinkish-brown shell at the stem end. You will also need to remove the stones. Tinned lychees are ready-stoned.

BLUEBERRY MUFFINS

MAKES 12
10 MINS TO PREPARE • 20 MINS TO COOK

*1½ tbls corn oil,
   plus extra for
   greasing
150g/5oz flour
65g/2½oz caster
   sugar
2 tsp baking powder
pinch of salt*

*1 egg
150ml/¼pt milk
50g/2oz blueberries
   or blackcurrants
butter, for serving
   (optional)*

1 Heat the oven to 200°C/400°F/gas 6. Grease a bun or muffin tin with corn oil.

2 Sift the flour, baking powder and salt into a bowl and stir in the caster sugar. In another bowl, lightly beat the egg, then stir in the milk and oil.

3 Add all the liquid to the flour mixture and beat until evenly mixed and smooth. Fold in the blueberries or blackcurrants.

4 Spoon the mixture into the tin. Bake for 15–20 minutes or until well risen and a fine skewer in the centre comes out clean. Serve the muffins hot, with butter, if wished.

INGREDIENTS GUIDE

Blueberries are the larger, sweeter and more succulent North American cousin of the bilberry. They have similar blue-black skins with a misty-grey bloom. Fresh blueberries can be bought in late summer but frozen ones are also available.

ZABAGLIONE

SERVES 4-6
25 MINS TO PREPARE • 20 MINS TO COOK

*8 egg yolks
50g/2oz caster sugar
75ml/3fl oz
   Marsala wine*

*cigarettes russes,
   tuile biscuits or
   langues-de-chat,
   to serve*

1 Put the egg yolks and caster sugar in a medium-sized mixing bowl and whisk them together until thick and creamy.

2 Gradually whisk in the Marsala wine, then place the bowl over a saucepan of gently simmering water and heat for about 15–20 minutes or until the mixture thickens, whisking constantly.

3 When the mixture has thickened enough for the beaters to leave a trail, pour the zabaglione into warmed serving glasses and serve immediately with cigarettes russes, tuile biscuits or langues-de-chat.

PLEASE NOTE

This dessert contains lightly cooked egg yolks, so should be avoided by young children, pregnant women, nursing mothers, the elderly and those suffering from immune deficiency diseases.

SERVING IDEAS

Marsala wine is the traditional ingredient used for zabaglione and is relatively inexpensive. However, if you prefer, you could substitute it with sweet sherry or Madeira, or even an orange flavoured liqueur such as Grand Marnier.

RASPBERRY MERINGUE NESTS

SERVES 4
10 MINS TO PREPARE

225g/8oz fresh raspberries
4 meringue nests
275ml/½pt double cream

1 tbls caster sugar
2 kiwifruit

1 Reserve 4 raspberries to decorate the nests and place the rest in a bowl. Crush the raspberries gently with a fork. Divide the mixture evenly between the four meringue nests.

2 Whip the double cream with the sugar until it stands in soft peaks. Be careful not to overwhip. Pile the cream on top of the crushed raspberries.

3 Decorate the top of the nests with slices of kiwifruit and the reserved raspberries.

VARIATIONS

This recipe could also be made in one large meringue case instead of several small ones. Meringue nests and larger meringue cases can be bought in large supermarkets and save a lot of preparation time.

INDEX